W9-AGU-847

SINGLE-

SESSION

SOLUTIONS

Single-Session Therapy

*Maximizing the Effect of the First
(and Often Only) Therapeutic Encounter*

SINGLE-SESSION SOLUTIONS

A Guide to Practical, Effective, and Affordable Therapy

MOSHE TALMON

ADDISON-WESLEY PUBLISHING COMPANY

READING, MASSACHUSETTS   MENLO PARK, CALIFORNIA   NEW YORK
DON MILLS, ONTARIO   WOKINGHAM, ENGLAND   AMSTERDAM
BONN   SYDNEY   SINGAPORE   TOKYO   MADRID   SAN JUAN
PARIS   SEOUL   MILAN   MEXICO CITY   TAIPEI

The material on pages 181–183 is from James Mann and Robert Goldman, *A Casebook in
Time-Limited Psychotherapy,* New York: McGraw Hill, 1982, 1982. Reprinted by
permission of James Mann.

The material on pages 176–178 is from Connirae Andreas and Steve Andreas, *Heart of
the Mind: Engaging Your Inner Power to Change with Neuro-Linguistic Programming.*
Moab, UT: Real People Press, 1989. Reprinted by permission of Steve Andreas.

The material on pages 172–173 is from Aaron T. Beck, *Cognitive Therapy & Emotional
Disorders,* New York: International Universities Press, 1976. Reprinted by permission of
the publisher.

Library of Congress Cataloging-in-Publication Data
Talmon, Moshe, 1950-
      Single-session solutions : a guide to practical, effective, and
   affordable therapy / Moshe Talmon.
            p.   cm.
      Includes bibliographical references and index.
      ISBN 0-201-63239-X
      1. Single-session psychotherapy.   2. Consumer education.
   I. Title.
   RC480.55.T348   1993
   616.89'14—dc20   93-11394
                                                         CIP

Jacket design by Ned Williams
Text design by Bruce Kennett
Production services by Julianna Nielsen, Sloane Publications
Set in 11-point Minion by B&W Typography

1 2 3 4 5 6 7 8 9 10-ARM-9796959493
First Printing, October 1993

Contents

Introduction

Jack is 42 years old, married to Kirsten, and the father of Jessica (age 5) and Tom (age 2). One Friday, he picked up Kirsten on his way back home from work. It was raining for the first time in months. The roads were slippery and visibility was poor. The car skidded and Jack lost control on the exit from the freeway to their neighborhood. The car crashed into the roadside guardrails. Kirsten was badly injured when her head hit the front window and she lost consciousness immediately. Jack had only minor bruises because the driver's side was equipped with an air bag.

After a month of intensive care and three operations, Kirsten started to recover and gradually regained most of her functioning. During that time Jack acted as a devoted father and husband. Jessica told him one night, "You are my superdad." And indeed, he was managing very well, attending to all the kids' needs while also going to work and standing by his wife at the hospital.

Shortly after Kirsten returned home, Jack became depressed and guilt-ridden. He was unable to concentrate at work and lost much of his normal appetite and ability to sleep. He was hoping to shake it off with his willpower and sense of responsibility for his family. Jack had never seen a psychiatrist, nor did he care to see one. Yet, the more he tried to talk himself out of the depression and guilt, the worse they seemed to get. After six months of efforts to shake off the bad feelings, he was still feeling miserable. Not only was Jack unable to go back to his old self, but now he was losing a sense of hope and control over his own feelings and life in general.

As Kirsten continued to progress rapidly toward complete recovery, Jack was becoming the sick one in the family. He finally agreed to consult Dr. Tyler, his personal physician and a longtime friend of the family. After a thorough check-up and several lab tests, Dr. Tyler called Jack to his office. "The good news is that there is nothing wrong with you physically. The bad news is that you are clearly depressed and psychologically shaken by the accident. I think you ought to see a psychiatrist."

Depression As an Act of Love

At that point, Jack decided to swallow his pride and ignore his mistrust of psychiatrists. "I guess I should do what Dr. Tyler suggested. I am becoming too much of a burden on all of you." At the recommendation of a friend, he called me and requested an appointment with a psychiatrist.

"I am a clinical psychologist, not a psychiatrist," I explained.

"What's the difference?" he asked.

"The main difference is that I don't prescribe medication. A psychiatrist is a doctor of medicine. I am a doctor of psychology."

"That's fine with me. The last thing I want is to take psychiatric drugs. But I have had it. And I just don't know what to do anymore."

The therapist needs to first understand and acknowledge the client's feelings, and then facilitate the positive traits that are submerged and can be activated. My first role was to recognize and give legitimacy to Jack's feelings. After listening attentively to his story during our session, particularly concerning his feelings following the accident, I said: "You are clearly depressed. You are feeling this way because you are a very caring, loving, and responsible husband and father. Your depression is your way of expressing to your family your regrets and sorrow for causing the accident."

I paused and then continued: "Your coming here today to see me is not only the right step at the right time, but also a wise and courageous step: facing your own feelings and going to a psychologist about it. It is a difficult step for anyone to take. I appreciate your willingness to take this risk and to be so candid with me, despite your initial fears and doubts about going to see a psychiatrist.

"Now, it seems to me that you are ready to recognize that none of us, including you, is perfect. Accidents, even very bad ones, happen to all of us at one time or another. Now that you have taken full responsibility for causing the accident you are ready today to go back to your regular self: being a responsible father and husband. Now, you can also begin to see the other side of the coin: The accident made you recognize how grateful you are to have Kirsten and yourself alive, and bless your kids for being so full of life and love. I am sure you want to find a renewed way to show them your positive feelings."

Jack was surprised and puzzled by my response. He told me later, "I was afraid you would scold me for stuffing down my feelings—that you would make me talk about all the traumas in my life—and then, tell me I need years of therapy to solve my unconscious problems."

Jack was seen for single-session therapy (SST). The art of therapy, in this case, was to facilitate change that can lead to a practical and relatively immediate solution. I reframed the depression as an act of love and caring, thus removing the self-perpetuating guilt and shame, and then formed an avenue to a solution by showing how this "act of care and love" could be expressed differently.

SST is not a one-shot, magic cure for all psychological problems. It is a new approach to therapy that was best summarized by Jay Haley, author, supervisor, and leading authority in modern psychotherapy: "SST makes us realize that therapy is still a new and surprising endeavor. We once assumed that long-term therapy was the base from which all therapy was to be judged. Now it appears that therapy of a single interview could become the standard for estimating how long and how successful therapy should be."

SST can get you "unstuck" from many psychological problems. It can help you stop destructive behaviors. It can free you from debilitating shame or fear. It can help you find the courage to make a long awaited decision or take action. It can give you a whole new angle on your situation. It can reassure you that you are *not* "losing it" or going crazy, and that soon you can go back to feeling, acting, or thinking like your old self, as Jack reported doing in a follow-up phone call, six months after his single visit with me.

No therapist should dogmatically limit his or her services to one session. His or her only concern should be to help you as quickly as possible. This can often be done in the very first session. When and if you need more time, you can resume therapy at any point, whenever it becomes necessary throughout your life cycle. At times, you may need therapy as a turning point at a crossroad; at such times you'll find one or a few sessions immensely useful. At other times you may want the therapist to walk with you along a certain path, thus requiring longer therapy. But perhaps this last approach will become the exception instead of the rule.

Consumer's Guide to the Briefest Therapy

Single-Session Solutions is written so that no one will have to fear psychotherapy and delay for years a solution to disturbing problems like depression, anxiety, impotence, poor communication with family, or low self-esteem. This book is written to make it both easier for you to get into therapy and easier and faster to get out of it. This is a consumer's guide to the briefest and most cost-effective therapy of all: single-session therapy. It is based on some very simple facts:

- All therapies start in the first session.
- Often one session is all that is needed.
- The first session tends to be the most important, powerful, and effective—regardless of the length of therapy.

The scientific and clinical bases for the phenomenon of SST were explained in detail in my first book, *Single-Session Therapy: Maximizing the Effect of the First (and Often Only) Therapeutic Encounter.* Some of the more technical information in that book I relay or allude to here.

Single-Session Solutions is for people contemplating the solution of psychological problems that result from feelings, thoughts, and actions in relation to themselves or others. It shows you how to take charge and make this problem-solving process shorter, safer, and less expensive than you ever imagined possible. You will learn the inside story of psychotherapy and why I came to believe that therapy need not be lengthy.

The book describes how single-session therapy is conducted. It outlines this alternative model for therapy, one that replaces the conventional model which has kept so many people fearful of therapists and therapy. It is based on psychohealth instead of psychopathology. It focuses on solutions instead of problems. It offers partnership between therapist and client instead of control, patronization, domination, and hierarchy.

In reading this book you will find out that in many cases the most cost-effective treatment is no therapy at all—as long as you are willing to be your own best therapist and learn the skills to do so. Self-therapy can be even better than single-session therapy. You can evaluate whether you're able to solve the problem yourself, or whether the help of a friend is necessary.

The first goal of this book is not to glorify therapy or therapists, it is to help you be your own best therapist. This idea should not exclude professional help. When you consider seeking the outside help of a therapist it should not be because your doctor sends you to a psychiatrist or because your spouse or boss hints you "need to see somebody." Outside pressure is not the best motivation for change.

Therapy, as presented here, is a highly collaborative, effective, and brief method for solving problems that have for too long hindered many people's development and sense of success. If you or somebody you care for needs outside help, this book will help you find the right therapist. Finding the right therapist means matching personalities and needs, understanding how therapy works, and realizing that it need not be lengthy. Finally, the book outlines the responsibilities of therapists and the ways you can maximize the effect of each and every therapeutic encounter, whether you are considering one session or are in the middle of open-ended therapy.

When a person recognizes a problem and makes a decision to take care of it, a powerful therapeutic process begins in his or her mind and body. Confronting a problem does not necessitate blaming oneself or anybody else. It only requires the desire to take care of it or to do something differently.

Single-Session Solutions is not a book about exceptional or outstanding people. Many people demonstrate considerable powers of spontaneous recuperation as well as the ability to resolve their own problems. Some people acknowledge their capacities and give themselves credit for them, while others keep ignoring them. Luckily most people can learn to see and emphasize their strengths.

When Diane called and told me her son was threatening suicide, she was scared and paralyzed. When I saw her two weeks later she was firm and confident.

"His threat pushed me up against a wall. I had no time to waste," she explained. "Shortly after I made up my mind to see you, I also confronted him. I first explained to him that I, as his mother, can't live under such threats. Then, I gave him an ultimatum. He has to shape up or move out. He chose to stay home. And this week I can see some very definite changes in his behavior."

Diane and her son required only one session of therapy because she understood the basic premise of productive therapy: The time for change is now, and nobody can help you better than yourself.

If you find it isn't possible to solve the problem without professional help, this book will guide you toward psychological help that is safe, brief, and inexpensive. Like many people, you may view psychotherapy or going to a psychiatrist as the equivalent of, or at least along the same lines as, being locked up in a "nuthouse" (remember Jack Nicholson in *One Flew over the Cuckoo's Nest?*), or of lying on the shrink's couch forever (remember Woody Allen in *Annie Hall?*). Many people who suffer from psychological problems share this view and consequently never seek treatment.

Achieving mental health can be a much simpler and more productive process than you have imagined. Dealing with psychological problems does not need to be a long and painstaking process. Contrary to conventional wisdom, it isn't necessary to spend a lot of time and money to get appropriate psychological help. The most common and cost-effective form of therapy is that of one session only; and when this is not sufficient, you will be guided on how to use a few more sessions (in most cases less than ten sessions) in order to use therapy successfully.

Achieving Mental Health Can Be Safe and Inexpensive

Regaining your mental health can be a safe, brief, inexpensive, and readily available process. The therapy you'll be guided to use in *Single-Session Solutions* is safe because it will not put you at risk of being locked up or forced into treatment; it will not start you off on a long, interminable road. It will not humiliate you, nor will it expose your dark secrets. It is safe because you will be in control of the process and its outcome.

The cost will be minimal. You do not need to attend seminars, buy herbs, or see a therapist for years in order to get healthier. If you decide, after all, that you do need outside help, I'll show you how and where to get it with minimal expense of money and time. You are likely to need only one to five sessions, which may cost you anywhere from nothing to a few hundred dollars.

With the skyrocketing costs of health care in general and mental health care in particular, governments, employers, and insurance companies have limited the number of psychotherapy sessions in most health care systems. For example, employment assistance programs (EAPs) geared to help employees with psychological problems limit them in most cases to three or five sessions. Health maintenance organizations (HMOs) provide pre-paid health care, yet often will limit therapy to six sessions. In fee-for-service settings, you and your therapist may desire open-ended therapy but the insurance company (or perhaps in the future, a national health care plan) will only pay for short-term therapy.

During the last three years I have devoted many hours to training thousands of therapists around the world how to conduct effective single-session therapy. Nevertheless, most therapists still prefer to take more time to get to know their clients and their problems. Each therapist has his or her own blend and style, and the field of psychotherapy is blessed with hundreds of different methods of doing therapy. I can only describe my way here, and guide you on how to be in charge of the length of psychotherapy, regardless of the therapist's expectations and method. The ultimate decision of when to start and when to end therapy should rest with you. When you act as an active and responsible consumer of therapy, you'll learn to set attainable goals, stay focused, and end therapy as soon as possible by utilizing the therapist's recommendations in your everyday life and enjoying the help of other agents of change such as a friend, lover, or sibling.

You have already started a process of self-examination. With the help of this book you will find out that many of the answers and "cures" are available without further therapy or cost. You'll work with your own common sense and intuition and you'll act within your own natural talent. In most communities there are plenty of mental health professionals employing many different effective therapeutic and counseling methods. If you ever reach a point where you need help, you'll be able to get it immediately, and in many more ways than one. If it doesn't work with one therapist, you can always try someone else.

I am not trying to persuade you to go (or not to go) to therapy. I will attempt to show you how to do it effectively either way; how to be your own best therapist or to get high quality and efficient professional help. Hopefully, after reading this book you will have a sense that you have more options and more control in the process of solving personal problems.

An Emphasis on Health Instead of Pathology

Single-Session Solutions presents a new and hopeful approach to solving psychological problems. I hope that you will find that the ideas expressed in this book offer refreshing new insights *and* a ring of truth that corresponds with your existing knowledge.

This book represents a new phase of psychotherapy, a shift that is taking hold in many places and in many people's minds. The emphasis on psychopathology is being replaced with a focus on psychohealth. Deficiencies are being replaced by abilities. Hierarchy is being replaced by partnerships and networking.

Introduction

Therapists and doctors are being replaced by self-help groups. The notions about a single objective and expert truth are being replaced by a multiplicity of options. Stress finally can be seen as a challenge, an opportunity for new learning, and not a reason to feel defeated or take Valium.

The basis for this book is a series of formal and informal studies of what can happen when therapist and client meet only once. I first wanted to know how often it happens, since I was educated to see therapy as a very long-term process. I surveyed 100,000 psychotherapy appointments in a large medical center in California over a five-year period, and later compared my survey with other studies and national surveys. Second, I followed up with two hundred clients of mine who had elected not to return after the first session (often against my advice). Third, I joined with two talented and experienced therapists, Drs. Robert Rosenbaum and Michael F. Hoyt, in sixty attempts to provide planned single-session therapy first mentioned on p. 4, where both the therapist and the client were aware of the possibility of SST but kept the option for longer therapy if and when indicated.

Who Benefits from SST

When we started our study of single-session clients, we assumed that SST would help only two groups of clients with mild problems: the "worried well," people who fear they are mentally sick but can be evaluated and reliably reassured that what they are experiencing may be hard or scary but is not crazy or sick; and the "psychologically shaken," those who, as a result of a recent traumatic or stressful event (like a car accident or a recent divorce), experience acute symptoms such as anxiety and depression but are capable of recovering within a short time after the incident. Much to our surprise, many severe, unexpected, and long-standing problems were dramatically helped in a single-session therapy: a man addicted to cocaine, a family afflicted by physical violence, an overweight woman who had tried every possible diet and failed with them all, and many more.

Therapy Myths

Some of the main obstacles in seeking psychological help are the myths and images that people have about so-called shrinks. How accurate are your own perceptions of psychotherapy?

What follows is a list of convictions about psychotherapy that many people hold. This book will show that many of those myths are inaccurate, or are at least elements of a specific model that is neither natural nor inevitable.

- When people suffer from psychological and mental illnesses they go to see "shrinks."
- Therapy takes a long time because psychological problems are buried in the unconscious and are rooted in forgotten early childhood traumas.
- The bigger and more long-standing the problem, the longer the required therapy.
- People who quit therapy before the therapist wishes them to are in denial about their real problems.
- More is better. Longer therapy will give you better results than short-term therapy because it's deeper and gets to the core issues of human dilemmas.
- For therapy to be effective, deep character changes must be accomplished.
- Therapy is long and hard work. There is no magic, no quick fix.

- Therapists are more objective and accurate than patients about the nature of the real problem and the treatment required.
- Good therapists will uncover the dark secrets of a person's life.

The facts are:
- Most people who face acute psychological problems never seek the help of mental health professionals.
- Among those who end up in a therapist's office, most do not wish to "be analyzed" or "lie on the couch" for a long-term therapy, as therapists do in their training. Instead of spending a lot of time on the past, most clients want to take care of the problem *now* and go back to their regular lives as soon as possible.
- Many come only once. On the average, they stay in therapy for three to six sessions. Clients wish to spend less time in therapy than their therapists wish they would.

Brief Therapy Research Findings

The myth that more, deeper, and longer therapy will inevitably offer better results is a hard one to break. Here is a brief summary of research findings that are rarely presented to the potential customer of psychotherapy. They are based on an extensive review of research comparing long-term with short-term therapy. Professor Bernard L. Bloom of the University of Colorado reviewed 460 references on this subject. Here are some of the findings:
- People who were hospitalized for brief psychiatric treatment (three to five days) have done as well as people with similar conditions who received extensive inpatient treatment (averaging sixty days). Many of the patients who were hospitalized for less time have done better in the long run—that is, they had fewer and briefer relapses that required repeated hospitalizations.

- People with similar conditions who were treated on an out-patient basis only (usually one fifty-minute session a week), improved as much and more than those treated in inpatient therapy (intensive program of at least eight hours a day of therapeutic activities in a controlled environment).
- One weekly session is as beneficial for clients as more frequent sessions (ranging from two to five times a week).
- Short-term therapy (defined as up to twenty sessions), is overall as effective as long-term therapy (a year and longer with an average of seventy-six sessions).
- Therapists who had longer and more extensive training (psychiatrists and psychoanalysts), did not get better results than therapists with shorter training (like social workers). Therapists who have undergone therapy themselves are not more successful than those who have not. Therapists who spent more time and money on their education and training (including their therapy) will charge more, but will not necessarily offer more for the money.
- Most stunning of all: In a series of studies I conducted with my colleagues, Michael Hoyt and Robert Rosenbaum, from 1987 to 1989 at Kaiser Permanente Medical Center, we found that clients who were seen for a single interview have done as well as those who stayed for a longer course of therapy. The single-session clients did not face simpler problems. Among the SST clients were heavy drinkers, abusers of hard drugs, and people faced with severe and stressful events such as violence in the family, death, and recent divorce.

This summary is not the result of radical, obscure, or exceptional research findings. These findings represent the common, everyday reality of psychotherapy services across America. As summarized by leading authorities in psychotherapy research, there is considerable cumulative evidence suggesting that brief therapeutic contacts make a significant and lasting clinical impact. The most clear-cut conclusion is that more is not necessarily better. Even if we take a more conservative view of these findings, we can safely conclude that briefer therapy will give you, the client, more therapy for your money and time. You will avoid the risk of large expenses for diminishing returns.

Enjoy and pay attention to your problem-solving capacities. Have fun with this book. You can read it in parts or as a whole. Take care of problems only when you are ready. Until then, the ideas you'll find valuable in this book can stay in a safe place in your mind, to be put into action whenever you wish and whenever you feel capable. Life is full of miracles and your mind is full of wonders and mysterious capabilities. I don't know which segment of this book will switch the light on for you. The ideas, metaphors, and examples in this book are presented as food for thought. When you make a shift in the way you look at a problem, you are likely to change your experience as well. Enjoy yourself. You are the main ally in your own success!

Therapy
Reconstructed

Psychotherapy, the modern and scientific method of treating psychological problems and mental disorders, currently treats and heals only a few of those who most need it. A national survey, released in February 1993 by Dr. Darrel Regier, director of epidemiological studies at the National Institute of Mental Health, found that about 52,000,000 Americans suffer from a psychological problem that is incapacitating in some way. (This survey was reported in an article by Daniel Goleman in the *New York Times.*) Only 8 percent of those with problems were treated. "It's a serious concern," admits Dr. Regier, "when one in five American men and women has a diagnosable psychiatric disorder, but receives no treatment for it." In short, most people, when faced with a psychological problem (let alone a psychiatric disorder), do not reach out for outside psychological help by a licensed psychotherapist (psychiatrist, clinical psychologist, or clinical social worker). This is true despite the fact that in most communities there is now a surplus of licensed therapists.

The need for psychological help is everywhere. Psychological problems are ever-growing with stress at work, troubled marriages, divorces, failures in intimate relationships, low self-esteem, and high rates of abuse (chemical, sexual, emotional and physical). Such problems are common among so-called normal people.

As a therapist, I am troubled by our failure to reach out to those who could benefit from psychological help. In times of sky-rocketing health care costs, we fail to provide what is potentially the cheapest and best way to improve health. Psychological help does not require surgery or expensive technology. Yet people are often more willing to subject themselves to medication with strong side effects and expensive surgery with high rates of complication and risk, than they are to ask for psychological help.

Martin Seligman and Aaron Beck of the University of Pennsylvania, leading authorities in studies on depression, indicated that 45 to 90 percent of depressed people are misdiagnosed by their family or primary care physicians. Their depressions are either never addressed or are treated with the wrong medications. A patient may tell the doctor of sleeping problems but not of depression and, as a result, the doctor may prescribe Valium or Halcyon. Such drugs are not only habit-forming but may deepen the depression as well. Depression weakens the immune system and thus may lead to many other illnesses that might have been avoided. The scientific evidence that depression can inhibit the effectiveness of the immune system was summarized by Joseph R. Calabrese, Mitchel A. Kling, and Philip W. Gold of the National Institute of Mental Health in Rockville, Maryland. The sad part is that most depressions can be treated effectively, safely, and quickly within a few sessions with a well-researched, safe, and scientifically-based cognitive therapy combined with, or without, anti-depressant medications.

On the other hand, many who put their trust in long-term therapists and enter in-depth therapy seem to never get out of it. My friend Woody has been in therapy all his adult life. By now, he has been in therapy for over twenty years. He sees a highly respected therapist who is also a professor and who teaches and supervises many other therapists. Woody is talented and knows how to take care of himself. He is very insightful about his own feelings and ideas. He succeeds at his work. He is creative and productive, and has published many books that have received rave reviews.

Despite all this, he is deeply troubled and unhappy. In fact, he is quite miserable and feels his life is going nowhere. Why? Because he continuously fails in his most significant relationships, particularly with women. He divorced his first wife after many years of miserable marriage. He quickly fell in love with another (married) woman. As soon as she divorced her husband in order to be with him, the new relationship went sour and now consists of endless fights and mutual disappointment.

In his therapy, Woody learned to understand himself, not others. He developed a great ability to retrieve and analyze his dreams but often ignored the most basic needs of his spouse and children. He is simply too busy and preoccupied with himself. He is dominated by his own story. When we get together he can analyze his private life for hours, often at the expense of the people right in front of him, including his children.

Most people still believe that people like Woody who stay in therapy forever are the typical therapy patients. And the "really crazy" ones seem, in our cultural imagination, to become prisoners or addicts of the psychiatric system, constantly under strong medications and going in and out of psychiatric facilities. They develop psychiatric careers instead of resuming normal life.

These are scenarios that most people naturally are wary of and wish to avoid. I wonder sometimes if by calling therapists "shrinks," clients mean that therapists shrink their pockets and their minds.

Modern psychotherapy has failed these patients in its most important role: to help people help themselves, to help them regain a sense of self-mastery and hope, and to help them go back to the business of life without undue dependency, years of psychiatric care, and very high expenses. The modern healers have done their patients a great disservice by promising more than they can deliver and by making people believe that therapists can be powerful enough to make life painless and risk-free. Many therapists sell the romantic idea that people can be 100 percent in control of their feelings, thoughts, and actions, thus writing and directing their life-scripts, controlling their environment and their experiences of it. It may be wiser for therapists to promise less and deliver more and for clients to be more aware of the potential as well as the limitations of what healers can do.

I initially decided to write this book in order to challenge the myths about psychotherapy and to make the use of therapy more accessible and attractive. The more I researched the subject, the more I realized that fear of psychiatrists, psychotherapy, and psychiatric labels has a profound basis in everyday practice (for a detailed description and discussion see Jeffrey Masson's *Against Therapy*).

Too many physicians and psychiatrists are trained to help only as long as their patients are helpless and sick. Status and financial incentives encourage a model of pathology and lengthy, sometimes drastic, intervention. The more severe and complicated the problem or illness, the higher the status of the professional is likely to be, and therefore, the greater his or her authority and power in the profession. Surgeons get the most status and money in medicine. Psychiatrists get the most status and money in psychotherapy. Recent studies show that the more specialized and higher the status of the physician, the more likely a patient is to get more medication, more surgery, and more expensive procedures, many of which are not necessary. For example, the patient who sees a private psychiatrist is more likely to receive medication, hospitalization, and more intrusive treatment—whether or not it is needed—than she or he would with a social worker in a community mental health service.

Problem Talk

The modern eye is well trained by television and film to notice what is wrong, tragic, conflictual, and sickening. Soon many get immersed in negative thinking and problem talk, two things that are particularly appropriate for the medical and psychiatric settings. Most people believe that when they come to a therapist they need to talk only about what's wrong, what's the problem, and what's bothering them. They think that this is what they are expected to do. By conveying only what is wrong and painful in their lives, many patients are taking a passive, dependent role, implying "I'll only tell you what's wrong and you'll be able to cure me."

Therapists and doctors in Western culture seem to thrive when people are ill and suffering. There is a saying that surgeons bury their failures, architects plant ivy on theirs, and lawyers visit theirs in prison. Psychotherapists' unsuccessful cases, on the other hand, return to see the therapist weekly, frequently for years. For relatively normal people, going to therapy can become a social event, a weekly mental massage, or, in more serious cases, an ongoing excuse not to assume full responsibility for their lives and relationships. It may provide a crutch—a cushioned arena in which to discuss conflicts that would best be discussed in the arena where the conflict originates. This safety may be important for a while but it can become an unproductive escape. Often, if a patient stays in therapy for more than approximately ten weekly sessions, she or he is more likely to continue unlimited, open-ended therapy for several years.

A person who has been encouraged to become a permanent patient is a desirable client for a therapist who seeks a steady and stable income in a fee-for-service, private practice setting. It is indeed a very lucrative position, combining the freedom of an independent professional with the stability of a salaried worker. The patient who becomes a permanent patient may do so as a technique to avoid meeting life's hardships and harsh realities. For people with relatively free schedules, regular therapy sessions can acquire the comforting characteristics of a ritual, a crutch, and a structural framework around which to plan their weekly activities. The role of patient also becomes comfortable and reassuring, enabling the transfer of responsibility and often decision-making powers to an "expert." In addition to ongoing support, time-unlimited therapy provides evidence, or at least the appearance, that patients are trying to do something about their problems and that someone is available, willing, and able to help. In today's world, it is hard to find such mutually ideal conditions anywhere else. A few conditions do require or are appropriate for long-term therapy. They are discussed in Chapter 6.

Therapy Abused

An inappropriate association has developed between psychological counseling and moral judgment. Many think of psychotherapy as a process through which the client is coerced or tricked into changing. These misconceptions are, for many, obstacles to confronting psychological problems.

Often an individual will label the problem of another as "psychological" or "psychiatric" as a way of implying that the other person is inferior, crazy, or wrong. Such labeling leads many people to deny having any psychological problems. When psychiatry and psychology are used by a person in a position of power to disqualify or judge another person, or even deny their freedom, something is seriously wrong. The tragedy is that most actions leading to forced psychiatric treatment are taken by well-meaning and even loving parents, friends, and spouses who are convinced they are acting for the patient's good.

In most cases, forced psychiatric treatment creates many more psychological problems than it solves. When one person is trying to dominate and coerce another into change, he or she abuses authority and uses psychological means as a form of moral judgment or emotional tyranny. This is not a therapeutic, helpful, or effective way to solve a psychological problem.

When parents ask me in my role as a therapist to make their son come home on time, I explain that if I thought it was my job to police their son's curfew, I'd go to the police academy and become a police officer. When a woman wants me to label her husband as having psychiatric problems so she can win in a custody dispute, I explain that if I'd wanted to be a judge of other people I would have gone to law school. A therapist should not act as a moral judge of other people's actions. Instead, she or he should serve as a catalyst for their clients' potential and ability to solve their own problems.

Using psychological means to force people to change is abusive. It is also one of the best ways to deter them from dealing with their psychological problems. Many people do not benefit from treatment because it is not initiated by themselves, but by another person or institution making threats or exerting power over them. Allen Frances and John Clarkin of Cornell University Medical College found that as many as 35 to 40 percent of psychotherapy patients continue treatment although they have a negative response or no response at all to therapy. The most obvious case is that of the so-called sociopath or psychopath—patients with antisocial or criminal behavior who are referred to treatment by the legal system after committing a crime. Another example is found among people labeled as alcoholics or addicts who enter treatment under threats of divorce or of being laid off from their jobs. Fifty percent or more of these clients will go through an expensive and lengthy treatment process, but soon after will go back to their old behaviors. It is hard enough for people to change old habits even when they want to. It is usually a waste of time and money to try to do so under pressure or threat from another. Many clients are smart enough to fake change so they can get out of treatment.

The Vocabulary of Human Deficit

Another disservice of modern psychiatry is the profession's willingness to lend its psychopathology-based language to people and institutions who wish to take control of the underprivileged. By using psychiatric labels and definitions to identify and separate certain segments of the population, or people with certain lifestyles or political beliefs, mainstream society can buttress its "normal and healthy" sense of itself. In many states it is legal to force psychiatric treatment on "out-of-control" people, lock them up, and subject them to strong medication against their will. For example, the fastest growing business in private hospitals is the use of psychiatric wards for teenagers whose parents find them hard to control.

The use of psychological jargon in everyday life can create problems as well. In the culture of pathologizing life problems, we are steadily bombarded with new psychiatric labels. Labels like *depressed, stressed, obsessive-compulsive,* and *paranoid* are now widely used by laypeople to characterize themselves or others. Consider the relatively new terms of "dependency" and "co-dependency," long expanded beyond alcoholism to include all other activities of life, such as eating, sex, shopping, work, exercise, and caring for loved ones. All these activities now have pathological terms to describe overdoing or underdoing them. When I was a child, my grandmother certainly stressed the importance of keeping things in the "right proportion." But she had no idea that this edict would become a feature of our common language, used against people to make them look sick. The danger, as Professor Kenneth J. Gergen of Swarthmore College noted in *The Saturated Self,* is that people get caught in a "continuous spiral of infirmity. If immersions in exercise, religion, eating, work, and sex are questionable or require professional treatment today, what will be left untouched tomorrow?"

The potential abuse of psychiatric labels is even greater when presented as scientifically based and as objective truth. The American Psychiatric Association devotes many efforts to describing abnormal behavior in clear, functional, and objective terms. Every few years they rewrite their diagnostic criteria for mental disorders. Fifteen years ago it was called DSM-II. In 1980, it was extensively revised into DSM-III. In the mid–1980s it was changed to DSM III-R; DSM-IV is due out in the mid–1990s. If, as mental health professionals, we are honest, we will abandon the idea that categories of mental illness and dysfunction are objective truths. In my view, it is neither true nor false that some people are schizophrenic, alcoholic, or depressed, or that some spouses are co-dependent. These are simply ways of thinking, talking, and trying to make sense of or categorizing our experiences.

The problem of the psychotherapy provider is even more complex if she or he has been educated, as I was, with the notion that psychiatry and clinical psychology are branches of medicine, where the main focus is to diagnose the underlying psychopathology. In medical tests it may be possible to quantify the range of normal function and clearly distinguish it from the abnormal. But a psychiatric diagnosis is deeply influenced by the practitioner's motives, culture, and ideology. Quite simply, I can justify treatment and find a psychiatric disorder in any person who seeks my help. In short, too many therapists are trained to justify their services by finding what is wrong with their patients.

Over-Treatment and Under-Treatment

Each treatment has its own side effects and risks. Therapy is no exception. The main risks in therapy are either over-treatment or under-treatment of the patient. More common is that of over-treatment, of not knowing when to quit therapy. The main risk of long-term therapy is that it will cause the very thing it set out to solve: Instead of becoming more independent and autonomous, a patient may become more dependent on the therapist, the psychiatric system, or parents who pay for treatment. If, for example, you have already entered ongoing therapy, the best way to deal with this risk is to ask yourself after a few sessions: Is there any progress? After three months or so, check to see if therapy is giving you less and less. Do you have little to bring to the session? Does therapy seem less important than other things you wish to do at that time? Does each session begin to seem like the last one or like a regular conversation with a friend? If so, it's time to terminate! If you find it difficult to decide, get the opinion of a friend or another therapist. In the end, the decision to terminate or not to terminate should be yours and not that of the therapist. Most therapists are reluctant to let go of patients, particularly if they pay promptly and are responsible and articulate. Be prepared for your therapist to advise you to terminate gradually, or even to suggest that your wish to terminate is a way to avoid a critical subject in the treatment. Early termination is rarely in the best interest of the therapist, especially if he or she likes working with you and makes his or her living this way. The final decision should rest with you. You know how much you have improved and how far you can go on your own. To avoid bad feelings, and to give yourself a sense of security, you may want to say to the therapist: "Let me try it on my own for a while and see how it goes. If I get stuck again, may I call you back?" You can give up your therapist, but don't give up on yourself. This is your investment in the most valuable asset of your life: yourself and your psychohealth.

The main risk of under-treatment is that you and the therapist may not have enough time to get to the bottom line, and you may settle for a bandage when you need major surgery. Or, you may quit when you need to progress, grow, and learn new skills. You are quitting for the wrong reasons if quitting is part of a pattern of not taking good care of yourself and your responsibilities.

Here are some ways to avoid the risk of under-treatment:
• Remind yourself that you can always go back to therapy whenever necessary.

- Arrange with the therapist a brief follow-up conversation (which can be done on the phone), or request that the therapist follow up with a phone call or letter as a reminder for you to reevaluate your progress.
- Be realistic. No one is ever cured for life, so if problems return or relief is short-lived, it's time to reevaluate your approach to solving the problem or it's time to go back to therapy.
- Don't look at it as an either/or choice. You can use one therapist for "troubleshooting" and consultation, and another for longer-term process therapy. There is more than one way to take care of a psychological problem. If it did not work out with a particular approach or person, try something else. When you are undergoing long-term therapy, or contemplating therapy to cure your "deep" psychological problems, keep in mind that most of our deepest problems cannot be solved; we can only learn to outgrow them or to live with them. One of the most important aspects in keeping therapy cost-effective is to learn the difference between what we can and cannot change.

Psychotherapy: The State of the Art

Psychotherapy is a healing relationship between a client (sufferer) and a therapist (healer). Psychotherapy aims to help solve a psychological problem and to overcome crippling, destructive, or hurtful emotions, behaviors, or relationships. In broader and more ambitious terms, it may help a patient to lead a fuller, more satisfying, and socially constructive life.

In primarily religious societies, such a process is based on religiomagical beliefs and healing rituals merged with religious rites. In modern Western societies, the process is based on the systematic application of a scientific understanding of human nature to the treatment of psychological problems and those who suffer from them. In its optimal use, psychotherapeutic knowledge is based on scientific findings while the therapeutic process is a refined art that is highly individualized, intuitive, and infinitely unique.

Different fields within psychotherapy tend to focus on one of three aspects of human nature: feelings, behavior, or thinking. In the psychoanalytic and psychodynamic theories, feelings, in particular, unconscious feelings, tend to be emphasized. The behaviorists, as their name suggests, emphasize actions and behavior. In the cognitive theories, thinking is emphasized. Within each of these theories, dozens of methods have been developed for treating problematic feelings, behaviors, and thinking. Many additional methods have been derived from these three major ones. In the past twenty years, more and more people have sought help as a result of specific interpersonal problems. As a result, many therapists now specialize in communication and system theories and they present themselves as marriage and family therapists or counselors. They see most psychological problems as resulting from interpersonal problems. In all of the major schools of psychotherapy, there are now well-developed methods to change a person's feelings, actions, and thoughts. Although most of these methods are based on conversation (the "talking cure") between the therapist and client(s), other methods exist that are based on other modes of human expression and communication, such as music, dance, painting, and drama. Using developments from recent findings in chemical, biological, and genetic studies, modern psychotherapy is making more and more use of a combination of talking and medication therapy for both medical (e.g. cancer, AIDS) and psychiatric (e.g. depression, anxiety) problems.

Attempts to integrate the different schools of therapy or to create a dominant, integrated method have not been particularly successful. Two models have gained more influence in recent years. The first is biological psychiatry, which suggests that many psychological problems are rooted in the brain and in genetic codes and therefore should be treated by medical doctors (psychiatrists, neurologists) in hospitals and medical settings. In the past, psychotropic medications were reserved for the most severe problems, such as schizophrenia, and had a bad reputation for producing severe side effects and controlling people against their will. In recent years, the development of new drugs combined with hungry consumers seeking a pill for every problem brought psychoactive drugs into many homes. Drugs like Valium for the treatment of anxiety, Prozac for the treatment of depression, Xanax for controlling panic attacks, and Ritalin for controlling hyperactive children, are all now widely known and used. The problem is that most psychoactive drugs have a similar fate: After a short period of glory when each is hailed as a miracle and touted as the new "in" drug, problems of overuse and side effects cloud the initial excitement. Nevertheless, thousands of schizophrenics can now function outside of psychiatric wards, and many people who previously suffered from years of debilitating and agonizing depression or panic attacks are now able to experience joy, energy, and relaxation.

The second movement is toward integration of body and mind. This movement offers a more interdisciplinary approach to psychotherapy. In medicine, this model suggests understanding psychological problems and mental illness using at least three disciplines of medicine: psychiatry, neurology, and immunology. This model focuses on the study of the body's natural forces that combat stress and illnesses. Outside of traditional medicine, the body-mind approach suggests the integration of old and new wisdom, Eastern and Western philosophies, and verbal and non-verbal therapies. It sees therapy as neither a science, nor a religion, nor an art, but instead as a combination of elements from all paradigms, emphasizing a holistic approach.

All of this suggests that the therapist of the future will be more versatile and flexible in the treatment of each individual. Post-modern treatment may use methods derived from the religious sphere (such as meditation), and artistic methods (such as music, drama, and drawing), and it may combine mental as well as physical activities. The problem in advancing body-mind therapy into the mainstream is that it often attracts charlatans and un-trained therapists who have difficulty in presenting research methods and findings that will be accepted by mainstream clients and providers.

What Works Best in Psychotherapy

The most consistent finding in psychotherapy research is that, overall, the different methods used in psychotherapy are all equally effective. The good news for the customer is that he or she doesn't need to research and learn every available method in order to select the right treatment.

Studies of the scientific foundations of psychotherapy and surveys on successful therapies like the ones conducted by Michael J. Mahoney of the University of Texas, and Lester Luborsky of the University of Pennsylvania Medical School, have repeatedly shown that clients rate personal interaction with the therapist as the single most important part of their therapy. Series of independently conducted studies, assessing a variety of outcome measures, indicate that aspects of the therapist's personality, such as warmth, are at least eight times more influential than the specific therapeutic techniques used or the therapist's preferred theoretical orientation.

What makes therapy work is rarely the particular method of psychotherapy for treatment of a particular symptom, but rather the choice of the right therapist—that is, a therapist who matches well with the client's personality and expectations. It is similar to looking for the right partner in a significant relationship. For example, would you work better with a direct and active therapist or would you prefer a soft-spoken, perceptive one? Are you looking for a charismatic leader or a supportive follower?

All the parochial wars between therapists about who is better than whom and about who holds the objective truth and key to mental health are totally irrelevant. After all is said and done, the features shared by all competent psychotherapists far outweigh their differences. Furthermore, they all are helpful sometimes to some people and not to others. Many popular self-help books suggest that the author's advocated approach is exclusively and particularly helpful in specific conditions.

The distinguished physician and psychologist, Professor Jerome D. Frank, headed the psychotherapy research group at Johns Hopkins University School of Medicine for thirty years. The group studied the ingredients that make up the effectiveness of psychotherapy's many different forms. A summary of its extensive research appears in *Persuasion & Healing: A Comparative Study of Psychotherapy* and *Effective Ingredients of Successful Psychotherapy*. It suggests that while each method of psychotherapy may use totally different names and rationales, the active therapeutic ingredients of all of them could be the same. What makes therapy work? What are the common ingredients that make therapy a useful and effective tool for a patient?

Frank identified the three basic R's of therapy as: relationship, revision, and ritual.

- A SECURE AND CARING RELATIONSHIP. The first and most critical issue in therapy is the therapeutic relationship. Other words have been used to describe this relationship: the "therapeutic alliance," "Eros," or "chemistry." The therapeutic connection may happen right away, as experienced in "love at first sight." At other times, the relationship may require a long process of building trust, intimacy, and mutual understanding. This is one of the reasons why using therapy to treat similar problems may range from one session to a lifelong affair. Eventually, only the patient can determine what is appropriate and sufficient.

  What makes the therapeutic relationship so powerful is the combination of trust and hope between people. A person needs to trust that the therapist is competent, genuinely cares about his or her well-being, and will do no harm. The hope is that the meeting of the patient's mind and the therapist's expertise will lead to improvements, while restoring self-confidence and maintaining self-integrity.

- REVISION OF THE PROBLEM. People go to see a therapist with a certain perception of the world and the particular problem they are having in it. The therapist offers a revised perception of the problem, its history, and the role the patient plays in it. Often what gets people stuck with a problem is not the thing itself, but the point of view they take. People often seek therapy not simply because they have a problem, but because they are demoralized about it. As the therapist listens to the client's story, she or he may hear overlooked facts and misunderstood evidence. Often when people are hopeless, they tend to remember and notice only the facts that support their bad feelings. The therapist may help with a fresh perspective. She or he can help a patient to acknowledge that even in the immediate situation there are some exceptions to the rule, and he or she might see small, yet significant evidence of progress toward a goal. Furthermore, she or he can help a patient to recall times in the past when things were different and can evoke a sense of hope, simply because if something worked once it may work again. A therapist may be able to redefine a problem so that it feels less overwhelming and more manageable. Together, patient and therapist can then formulate some small steps toward reaching a goal. Such steps may offer a sense of progress that will in turn strengthen a sense of hope. The feedback a patient gets from his or her therapist during, or at the conclusion of, the session is successful when it clarifies the nature of the problem as well as what can be done to deal with it.

- ACTIVE ENGAGEMENT IN THE RITUAL OF HEALING. The therapist gives or engages the patient in a ritual. Such a ritual can take many forms. For example, it may help the patient to openly express strong emotions in a safe environment. It may provide a patient with permission and a format to act on a thought or feeling long dormant. It may facilitate a patient's faith and hope by providing an affirmation or visualization in order to pass beyond the point of being "stuck." A nice example of such a ritual is told by Michael Mahoney of the University of Texas in his book *Human Change Processes.* An older woman came to therapy feeling tired of being leaned on as the "strong one" by her family and friends. The ritual aimed to "lighten her load." She filled her daughter's old Girl Scout backpack with heavy rocks. Each rock represented the demands placed on her by a different individual. Each afternoon she put on the backpack and walked more than a mile to a special place where she found she could be alone. Day by day, one by one, she removed a rock, spoke out loud about her unwillingness to carry that person's demands any longer, and threw the rock away. Then she set the backpack to another use. Now it was to carry little treats for herself: books, and treasures that she found on her daily walks. Good therapy can provide a meaningful ritual to transform a bad or hurtful experience into a good or positive experience or into a challenge.

The active ritual is the suggested solution to the presented problem. Both patient and therapist actively participate in the implementation of the solution. Both believe it to be the means of restoring a sense of well-being and health. Sometimes such a procedure includes more dramatic rituals such as hypnosis or medication. More often, it simply provides the patient with permission to let go of the problem or abandon the complaint. The therapist uses his or her authority to give the patient that permission. The session may serve as the occasion for relinquishing the symptoms the patient is ready to give up.

The ritual solution can be minimal or it can be symbolic by providing a useful metaphor so that a problem can be looked at differently. Or, it may offer encouragement to keep doing what is right for the client—after figuring out what that may be. Or, it may help to develop a trusted relationship with a therapist in order to correct traumatic and pathological relationships in the past.

The ritual solution tries to accomplish one or more of three goals:
- The first goal is to strengthen mutual interest and hope in improving a patient's condition and to establish trust that this

joint venture will be beneficial. It should maintain and further inspire a patient's expectation of help. Sometimes merely the name of a therapeutic agent or procedure mobilizes a client's hope of relief. For example, if a patient expects a pill to do the trick, a placebo may be all that is needed. If a patient expects hypnosis to do magic, the therapist can offer a simple relaxation exercise but substitute the word hypnosis for relaxation. This is not so much an indicator of the power of a therapist's tricks and magic as it is evidence of the power of a client's hopes and faith in therapeutic relations and in change. Thus, a client's role in the success of the therapy is not as passive as he or she may assume. As educated and active consumers, people involved in therapeutic rituals must link their hope for improvement to the process as well as focus on the outcome the patient and therapist agreed to work on. And both must trust that the ritual can provide the desired outcome. Therefore, for example, no one should agree to hypnosis if he or she fears it will inspire loss of control or performance of foolish things. No one should take medication if he or she is worried about side effects or addictive quality. And as much as a client needs to trust the therapist and understand his or her own role in the success of therapy, the therapist also needs to know about the client so she or he can develop the necessary faith and trust in the client's ability to use the procedure well.

- The second goal of using rituals is to provide a new learning experience. Therapeutic learning can be more than cognitive learning alone. Such learning is experiential in both emotional and practical matters. If a person's emotions are aroused as he or she faces the problem or tries a new way of dealing with it, not only will this teach the client that he or she can survive intense feelings, but it will also make change more real and believable. By taking a problem one step further than talking about it—by ritualizing it—the patient puts it into action and realizes his or her feelings about it. If a patient is not sure of himself or herself, the safety of the session can offer a chance to experiment and rehearse. For example, a client may role-play and rehearse a request for a salary raise from a boss or play out a difficult yet necessary confrontation with a parent.

• The third goal is that the ritual solution should provide opportunities and incentives for a ripple effect beyond the presented problem or temporary, short-lived solution. It can be achieved simply by the fact that one success may breed another one. An effective solution can be provided when the therapist's suggestion captures the essence of the client's story, thereby working its way more effectively into the rest of his or her life.

The Role of Hope in Healing

Favorable expectations generate feelings of optimism, energy, and well-being, and therefore promote healing. Faith in the therapist may be healing in itself. In its most basic way, therapy is a process of exchange between client and therapist. A client comes to therapy hopeless and doubtful about his or her ability to solve a problem. He or she places hope in the therapist and the therapist rekindles that hope. Hope can be defined as a perceived possibility to achieve a goal. There are some simple ways in which the therapist can arouse hope or at least offer cues that spark a light at the end of a dark tunnel.

A therapist can outline a course of action or prescribe medication or suggest a task that is associated in the client's mind with taking care of the problem. The "catch" in the role of hope is its close association with expectations. Expectations can be negative or unrealistically high, resulting in negative outcomes or the creation of high stakes. And if the therapist seems to fail the client, the client will of course be angry with the therapist. In a study of negative expectations, reported by Norman Cousins, a group of patients who feared drugs and distrusted doctors was prescribed an inert pharmacological substance (a placebo), yet they developed severe reactions including nausea, diarrhea, and skin eruption.

Hopes can soar higher as intervention grows more dramatic. When a client is desperate, he or she is ready to do whatever is needed and may place all hopes in a single act. An example could be medical surgery. In an experiment reported in the British medical journal *Lancet,* a surgical procedure aimed at increasing blood supply to the heart was performed on every other patient in a series; a mock operation was done on the alternates. The surgeon gave patients in the mock operation anesthesia and incised their chests without touching the artery. The result was the mock operation proved to be just as effective as the real one.

The more severe the problem, the higher the pressure on the therapist to take more dramatic measures. Such measures often present more risks. A competent therapist evokes and fosters hope, while helping the client realize that reliable expectations and realistic goals are the best bet in trying to achieve a goal.

Placebo Therapy

Placebo is another form of therapy. The therapeutic value of the placebo depends on the symbolic message and not on the specific agent or substance used. Medical as well as psychological problems are often treated effectively by the symbolic ingestion of hope via placebos. Clients respond more positively to placebos when the disorder has an emotional component like high anxiety or chest pains. A client may be further helped by a placebo if he or she tends to depend on others, and tends to accept and trust others in their authoritative role. Anxiety and depression are the most common feelings people have in crises, and they are also the feelings most responsive to placebo treatment.

The way in which hope influences a client's condition does not depend solely on the client. The expectation, attention, and hopes of the therapist and of others will strongly affect a client's response. As one of my clients said to me, "You were so convinced it was going to work, I just could not let you down."

If a client experiences the therapist as caring, supportive, and competent, he or she is more likely to respond to the placebo effect in therapy. The Finnish physiologist I. Kojo argues that placebos should be used intentionally, especially with treatments and drugs that have more direct physiological and pharmacological effects. He suggests that the placebo effect can be more general and long-lasting than effects caused by more specific agents.

It is important to note here that placebo treatment can be dangerous if it is used as a mode of deception because it may undermine the most important element in therapy: trust in the client-therapist relationship. Second, while hope can relieve distress and pain it should not replace addressing the problem that led to distress in the first place.

The relief you as a client experience as the result of your hope gives you sufficient moral support to face all your problems with some degree of fortitude. In short, it can be the kind of "beginner's luck" you need to go on with the process and "take care of the rest" with a higher level of self-confidence.

I discuss here the role of hope in therapy at some length because I have seen over and over again, in research findings as well as in my practice, how expectation colored by hope and faith becomes a major therapeutic force. It is particularly true with single-session therapy and for those who come to seek outside help because of a crisis or as a last resort. Because they are positioned on some threshold, clients are very perceptive and responsive to the therapist's suggestions.

As a patient, you need to pay close attention to your hopes and expectations and make sure they match your choice of therapist. If you want help now and hope that one or a few sessions will be sufficient, pick a therapist who believes the same.

The Therapist's Setting and Status

The place where a client meets a therapist should be a special place of healing. Religious healing rites are conducted in temples or sacred places. Secular therapies take place in an office, clinic, or hospital. The setting should, first of all, provide safety. Within its protective walls a client can freely express himself or herself; he or she can dare to reveal aspects often concealed from others. Clients should know that no harm will come to them during their session, and that when they leave the setting everything remains confidential; there will be no consequences in the outside world from what was said or done during the session. The setting should reinforce a client's expectation that the therapist is a well-trained and competent expert in the field. Evidence of that may be deduced from the therapist's diplomas, photographs, bookshelves, impressive desk, and his or her presence and bearing. Clients may find that other elements of the setting influence positive or negative expectations. These include the waiting room, paintings on the wall, and the therapist's clothing or general style.

The therapeutic power of sympathetic listening by a prestigious figure is undeniable. When we conducted the follow-up phone calls to single-session patients treated in Kaiser Permanente Medical Center in Hayward, California, we were surprised to find how much patients appreciated and even benefited from this brief telephone contact. "I know how busy you must be. It means a lot to me that a doctor like you cared enough to remember me and called to find out about how I am doing so long after the session." When asked what caused the changes, the most common answer was that the opportunity to get together and talk it all out, combined with the feeling that the doctor cared enough to listen, was the main reason for the changes that followed.

As reported by Jerome and Julia Frank, a medical student from Johns Hopkins University who had very little knowledge of psychotherapy helped, in a single session, a woman who suffered from the delusion that her nose was growing bigger and would eventually grow over her mouth. She didn't want nor did she ask for psychotherapy. She wanted plastic surgery and consulted a plastic surgeon, who referred her to a psychiatric clinic. The medical student doing his rounds in psychiatry was assigned to the case. He listened to her complaints for about an hour and a half. She left the session unconvinced, still insisting on an operation for her nose.

However, a week later she called the medical student to tell him that she felt much better and was resuming outside activities after a long period of being practically housebound, afraid that others could see her growing nose. She explained "the nose was only a little thing." A follow-up phone call eight months later revealed that she had continued to progress. When asked what had helped her, she replied: "The doctor had compassion for me. I wanted to talk and he let me talk."

It is possible that this was the first time she received so much sympathetic attention from a person of high status. This student was able to listen without agreeing that she needed surgery. And he didn't rush to diagnose her as psychotic—after all, she had delusions—and make her into a psychiatric case. He offered therapeutic and helpful attention because of his ability to limit himself to listening. If the student had argued with the woman about the surgery or tried to convince her to check into the psychiatric unit, this episode could have quickly turned into a fiasco, and the attention might have provided further support for the maintenance and intensity of her symptom. In short, therapeutic listening is often the wisdom of silence and restraint on the part of the therapist.

The personal problems amenable to therapy are those that happen as a result of disharmonies or imbalances within people or among people. Good therapy may help a person:

- reduce or overcome distress;
- function better in personal relationships and at work;
- increase self-esteem and sense of control over self and surroundings.

What the therapist does or says in therapy aims to enhance morale by challenging maladaptive patterns of behavior and perceptions and encouraging more successful ones. When therapy succeeds you as a client may—in addition to solving or coping with your problem—experience an increased sense of inner freedom, capability, and satisfaction with life. If you are ready to take care of business now, therapy is going to help you immediately.

Therapy usually takes the time allotted for it, no matter the severity of the problem.

Regardless of therapy's positive potential, as long as psychiatrists and psychologists agree to treat people against their will in locked psychiatric units or to testify in courts about who can stand trial and who can have custody of the children, and as long as therapists encourage only long-term, open-ended treatment, people will suspect therapists' motives and the misperception will continue. As a result, many people will be quick to suggest that somebody else—not them—needs a "shrink." The next chapter deals with relinquishing this tendency by addressing the more personal questions involved in seeking outside psychological help: Why should I go, when should I go, and whom should I see?

How to Begin Successful Therapy: Attitude, Timing, and Matching

Rick and Sally have been married for three years and have a one-year-old, a lively and healthy baby named Sam. They both love him dearly. A nice picture, if you will, of a normal, young family.

Both parents have demanding careers. In the evenings they are both tired. Sam has not seen his mom and dad all day and squeezes out all the attention he can get. He clings to Sally and does not let his parents talk to each other or do anything else. When he finally falls asleep after 9:00 P.M., Rick and Sally are exhausted and tense. They both need to unload the tension and relax. They look to each other for help. But it just doesn't work that way. A small disagreement turns into a nasty and loud argument. Rick blames Sally. Sally feels Rick doesn't understand her. They both feel stuck and angry. It is as if all their love, support, and understanding have vanished.

After more than a few such nasty arguments, Sally, tearful and helpless, says: "We've got to see somebody. We can't go on like this."

"What do you mean, see somebody?" Rick replies in an angry and defensive tone. "I'm not crazy and I don't need to see a shrink. If you have a problem, you go and see one. Besides, this is our private life and nobody else's business."

Why is the idea of seeing a psychotherapist so threatening to Rick? And Sally can't even say it straight and uses "somebody" instead of "psychologist" or "psychotherapist." When Rick uses "shrink," he suggests something derogatory.

Why is it so much simpler to seek the help of a physician when we have a physical problem or consult a lawyer when we can't solve a legal problem ourselves? Each of us may have slightly different reasons to avoid psychotherapy. In Rick's case there are several reasons. He believes:

- if he sees a therapist, it means he is crazy;
- going to see a therapist would be like confessing that he is inept, immoral, or at fault;
- private matters should stay private; telling private problems to and discussing intimate "secrets" with a stranger is forbidden in some cultures or just difficult for a person who has never done it before.

Let's examine some common misperceptions of therapy and the actual reality of psychotherapy practice.

"Only crazy people go to see a shrink."

One of the major reasons so few people benefit from psychotherapy is the myth that a person has to be somehow out of his or her mind or crazy in order to see a therapist. The argument goes further to imply that complaints (or psychological problems) are all imaginary and are not real. "Not real" means that a person would stop feeling bad if he or she just effectively summoned the will to do so, or that a doctor found nothing medically wrong and recommended a psychiatrist as a last resort, saying "it's all in your head."

In fact, most of the people who seek therapy are not sick or crazy. Often they are the more caring, stronger, and better functioning members of their families. They often come to therapy because they have more courage to face the problem; have better reality testing—they recognize the problem and take action to correct it; and are more responsible and caring—they wish to help another member of the family who is in trouble. The paradox of therapy is that the very fact that a person recognizes a problem and decides to take care of it by calling a therapist is the most clear evidence that he or she is functioning normally. The ordinary reality of most people is that they are always faced with some stresses and problems. When they can't solve these on their own, they seek outside help. If they ignore problems for too long, or pretend that what is there is not a problem, or invent a new reality to cover it all up, then they are well on the way to a state of craziness. In short, calling a therapist to get help in solving a problem is not only perfectly normal, it can be wise, resourceful, and productive.

"How can somebody help me if I can't help myself?"

This is a key question that I often hear, primarily from my male clients. Think about the study of the human brain. We know so little about the mysteries of the human brain, despite the great effort and expense devoted to brain research. One can assume that there is only so much the human brain can learn about itself. Likewise, there is only so much that we can see and do in regard to our own lives, particularly when it comes to intimate and personal matters. The more intimately we are involved with a personal problem, the more we lose the perspective necessary to assess it. For example, I tend to make mistakes with my own kids, although I can easily help other parents when they have the very same problems with theirs.

Everybody gets discouraged and worried at times. When that becomes one's dominant emotional framework, it may be time to seek treatment. No one can solve everything alone. Worse yet, at times, attempts to solve a problem only make us feel worse. In addition to having the problem, we feel demoralized and helpless.

"Can't I get the same help from a wise friend, grandparent, or a lover?"

Generally speaking, we can and do get much help, support, and useful advice from family members, friends, and lovers. A person who has religious faith or strong and healthy family ties, or a strong community of supportive people, will be in less need of therapy. People who are part of a well-structured social system and have clear values may be less in need of therapy.

Postmodern life requires frequent transitions. For better or for worse, the postmodern Western world is characterized by mobility and diversity, a lot of stimulation, weaker family ties, and lack of a stable social matrix. These factors often produce confusion, loneliness, separation, and fragmentation. A young adult may have left the parental home but find it hard to establish stable relationships or a career identity. Later on in life, after the loss of a loved one through death or divorce, this person may feel lonely and depressed again. When he or she overcomes this and falls in love with another person, he or she may soon encounter the complex problems of blending two lives or even two families into one.

"But why should I go to therapy? It's your problem, not mine."

This is a very common reply parents get from their children and wives from husbands. Many men have problems with the idea of going to therapy. They may consider therapy a threat or a waste of time. In the first ten years of my practice as a psychotherapist, the vast majority of my clients were women. Some men are afraid to lose control and feel that therapy will cause them to do so. Others are afraid of being labeled by some psychiatric term. For typical men, psychotherapy is about "women's stuff" (feelings, gossip, the private sphere) and is not very practical. Most of the men I see in therapy deny having any problem and come in at the request of others.

Therapists value talking, listening, understanding, feeling, and support: all very well understood and enthusiastically embraced by women, or at least by the conventions of "femininity." Therapy for the most part is talking a "women's language," which has kept many troubled men away from—even hostile to—therapists. Yet, women's troubles do not happen in a vacuum or because of isolated worries, nor are they innate only to women. Most often women come to therapy when they have troubles as mothers, as wives, as daughters, or as employees-citizens (in relation to men who have authority).

As a therapist, I see no point in telling a man he has a problem when he sees none. So, what can be done?

"I can't get my husband and kids into therapy, although we clearly have marital and family problems to solve. What can I do to bring them in?"
I have talked to many women who did go to therapy themselves, but found they could not convince their husbands to join them. One said: "It really takes two people to make a marriage work. Without his help, I can stay in therapy for years and nothing will change in his attitude. It may even get worse as a result of my going to therapy, because we grow apart from each other." A

similar dilemma exists when a troubled teenager feels insulted and becomes even more hostile when a parent suggests therapy.

In order to invite husbands or teens to join therapy, I first convey to them that I need them to come because they can help me to understand the situation better. I say I'm not interested in who has the problem. I want to know who has the solutions. In the therapy room, I am seeking agents of change, not blaming troublemakers. And besides, I explain, they may need to come only once.

If men and boys can understand that therapy is not about blaming them and that therapy is a practical and useful way to solve problems, they are more likely to join therapy. If I feel that the family member who called to seek therapy is angry and frustrated with a child or spouse, I personally extend the invitation to other family members. If, for example, you are worried that the idea of therapy will rub your spouse or children the wrong way, you may want to try the above approach or ask the therapist to give them a call. Therapists should know how to sell their trade.

Since my work with single-session clients became known, I get many more inquiries from men who now see that therapy can be brief, practical, and effective. Therapy that is more action-oriented and less based on listening and feelings may suit the conventions of traditional masculinity better. Women who want their spouses to join them in family or couple therapy may have better luck talking them into one session.

As a result of the way I present therapy to my clients, I now see many people who never agreed to see a therapist before. They have taught me that the human struggle to be independent and to maintain one's integrity and pride is not mere "denial" or "self-deception." More often than not, it is a powerful and creative force that constantly searches for better solutions and changes.

Even illusions and denial are necessary for coping with the complex and multiple realities of postmodern life. People wish to help themselves without undue outside intervention. This approach is much more healthy and appropriate than I could ever have realized from the limited view of a therapist who only sees people who are more amenable to the conventions of long-term therapy. It is important to respect the choices that loved ones are making. They may want to solve the problem but not in the same way as the person who initiated therapy does.

From the point of view of the client, three basic elements determine the effectiveness of therapy: **attitude, timing** of therapy, and **matching** between the client and the therapist. Let's examine each of the three elements.

A Question of Attitude

The attitude brought into the first session will do more than just predict its success. It will determine the clients' self-confidence as well as their faith in any future help they may need when and if they get stuck again. The personal qualities and attitudes brought to the therapy will have greater effect on its success than the technique the therapist uses.

Let's say you are someone who comes to therapy as a favor to your spouse, parents, or employers, or because you simply want them to stop nagging you. Rarely does much good come of therapy that is initiated this way. I once agreed to see a 55-year-old man because his wife felt he was an addictive gambler and threatened to divorce him unless he went to therapy. He, being a devoted Catholic, did not want the divorce and came to see me. He explained that gambling on horse races had been his favorite hobby for many years, and denied that this was an addiction. He claimed that he gambled once a week, that he bet a small amount, and that overall, he won as much as he lost. He clearly did not see it as a problem but rather as an enjoyable hobby. I said to him, "Since you are here so your wife will not divorce you, we may be able to find ways to improve your marriage so your hobby will not be a threat to your marriage." He replied, "My marriage is perfectly fine." I tried several other joint and individual sessions to find an agreed-upon problem to work on. The wife agreed only on the need to change her husband and the husband only agreed on the need to change his wife. It was clearly a bad reason and bad timing for therapy. A few years later, the younger son of the family was arrested for an attempted robbery. Then the wife and husband were able to agree on a problem—the son's crime—that needed to be dealt with, and this agreement gave therapy both a focus and a common purpose.

The most helpful attitude is recognition that therapy is not about who is right and who is wrong, but about the personal wish to face a problem and experience success in attempts to solve it. Often people fixate on one and only one solution. They try the same strategies again and again. They put their best efforts into finding a solution only to see matters getting worse. Brief therapy can be useful in order to find the right solution or to make the right decision, but it can also help a person stop doing something that simply does not work.

Therapy can also be viewed as a safe place to open up and consider new options. Here a person can feel free to express forbidden thoughts, release pent-up emotions, and experiment with new ways of behaving and relating without fear of failure or consequences. But watch out: Some people use the safety of therapy to complain about others or about life in general. Complainers waste their time and money by going to therapy. It may even worsen their situation if the therapist uses his skills of understanding, empathy, and patience. Complainers use the support and empathy of the therapist as a substitute for doing something about the problem. The client takes such support as evidence that she or he is right and therefore does not need to change. The times when a person mostly wants to complain about a spouse, a boss, the President, or anybody else, are bad times for problem-solving therapy. It may turn out to be only a venting or complaining therapy.

Instead of using therapy as the place to vent or complain, a person may want to consider meeting with friends who are sympathetic and supportive. For those who feel that they should pay for a sympathetic ear, they can offer to pay for the coffee, the meal, or the vacation site, where both parties may share a therapeutic conversation and safe environment.

Thomas A. Edison lost his laboratory in a fire that destroyed years of hard work worth millions of dollars and he had no insurance.

"What in the world will you do?" he was asked.

"We will start rebuilding tomorrow morning," replied Edison.

The loss of his laboratory did not destroy Edison nor did it make him depressed. Edison was a happy man who used problems to create better solutions. He confronted his problem with a sense of purpose and direction. He didn't wait for somebody else to assume responsibility for his misfortune. He did not blame himself or others. He simply wanted to be part of the solution—rebuilding. Edison's reaction exemplifies all the elements of an effective and healthy approach to confronting a distressing problem:

1. See the problem as a challenge.
2. Confront it squarely.

3. Focus on available solutions.

4. Don't put it off. Be part of the solution now.

When you confront a psychological distress or problem from the view that you do so in order to be part of the solution, you will find it an interesting and even empowering challenge instead of a threat to your sanity or reputation.

Timing

The ultimate test of the success of any form of therapy is whether or not a person can utilize or sustain the changes achieved in therapy. Therefore, the best time to come to therapy is when you, the client, are really ready to do something about your life, and if need be, do it on your own. The key to success in therapy is timing. Are you ready for change now?

Ask yourself "Why now?," and you are likely to find that there is a particular stress or recent event related to your decision to seek therapy. Most of the stresses that bring people to therapy involve interpersonal problems like family or work-related conflict. Therapy will be more helpful to you when you can identify a link between the problem and your interpersonal relationship and/or current stress. For example, you may recall that you started to lose sleep and feel anxious shortly after you were laid off from your job. On the other hand, when your problem is isolated from and unrelated to any event or relationship, your therapist is more likely to view it as a character fault or immutable personality trait. In such a case the therapist will see more reasons for long-term therapy and may be less optimistic about your rapid improvement. After all, changing your basic personality is more complex and difficult and suggests longer treatment. In reality all problems have personal and interpersonal components as well as earlier and more recent contributors. The more you recognize about the current stressor and the interpersonal elements, the shorter and more effective the therapy can be. Tell your therapist about the context of your problem. For example, if you come to therapy because you feel insecure, tell your therapist where, when, and with whom you did feel secure. Try to differentiate between the context where the problem presented itself as well as the times, places, and people where it did not. Be concrete and give examples. You and your therapist may realize that you don't have just one self and one level of self-confidence. For example, I feel very secure working with my clients and very insecure when I have to fix my car or an electric problem in my house.

You can determine your level of readiness by asking yourself:

- Are you aware of any role you play in the problem?
- How fed up are you with the present problem?
- Are you ready to take the necessary action or do you still need to just think and talk about it?
- Are you ready to assume personal responsibility for your part in the problem?
- Are you ready to let go of the guilt, blame and the "poor me" attitude right now?

The best timing is when it hurts too much. There is something that is very humbling and human about facing our failed attempts. It is in that very moment when "we can't take it anymore" that a truly significant and transformative change can take place. It is similar to near-death or near-total-defeat experiences that allow a new life or new experience to emerge. This profound turning point was beautifully described by Julie, a young woman who became blind as a result of diabetes. "Blindness taught me to see, and death taught me to live," she said (reported by the physician Bernie Siegel in *Love, Medicine & Miracles*). Facing reality is a powerful force in creating a turning point. Our most painful feelings have a purpose. I attended the births of my children, which were the most profound experiences of my life. At each birth, it was my wife's screaming that she couldn't take the pain anymore that brought the baby into the world in a matter of a few minutes. My wife said later: "When you feel this horrible pain you think to yourself, what in hell is this pain for? You need to remind yourself that this is your baby trying to come out to the world."

The moment of "pain before birth" is the right moment to enter therapy. The therapist is there to support, coach, and facilitate what is a perfectly normal process. The pain and fear may block people from realizing that this is a pain that could be instructive and purposeful.

When my father was diagnosed as having leukemia, a form of blood cancer, neither he nor any member of the family ever called the illness cancer or leukemia. Naming this illness cancer, for all of us, was equal to a death sentence we were totally unwilling to accept. My father was only 58 at that time and none of us were ready for his death. Until the day he died, we never openly acknowledged that he had cancer. He was sick and needed to stay in bed or the hospital. This was the extent to which we were willing to face the problem.

A year after he died my mother developed breast cancer. Now, we were ready to face the problem differently. The pain and fear of cancer and the loss of our father had awakened us all. My mother was a fighter and the only parent we had left. All of us, the three children, were now young adults living away from our mother's home. Somehow we had learned the lesson from my father's cancer. We openly called my mother's illness cancer, and treated it as a great challenge for us all. Mother changed her diet and her lifestyle and started living a fuller and healthier life. She became a vegetarian, learned to swim, developed new pleasurable hobbies such as growing indoor plants, traveling to nature sites, and listening to music. We opened up to her and became much closer. In the last years of her life we talked and did many more things together than ever before. We did not deny the diagnosis, but we did defy the verdict (cancer = death). The critical question was not how long she would live, but what each of us made of each and every day she was around. We all were awakened to living better and fuller lives as the result of her cancer. She died at the age of 78, seventeen years after she got cancer. She died at home and was independent and coherent till her very last days.

At what point in trying to solve a psychological problem will you decide to see a therapist? Each client has his or her threshold, beyond which outside help becomes necessary. I always ask my clients "Why now?," and these are the most common explanations I hear:

"Because I have tried everything and nothing works."
What have you tried? Here is a list of some of the things people do before going to a therapist:
- They try to solve their problems by themselves.
- They seek a friend's advice.
- They talk to their pastor/rabbi/spiritual leader.
- They read articles or self-help books.
- They try to ignore the problems or forget them.
- They try to place the responsibility or blame on others.
- They go to an internist or the family doctor with some physical manifestation of the problem.

At times, you may feel temporary relief. At others, you may get what you want or need from one of the above. That's okay. Don't fix it when it works. Only when you have tried it all and nothing seems to make the problem go away do you end up at a therapist's office. Some people go to a therapist only after a few friends have made the suggestion that you better "go see somebody."

"Because I reached a breaking point."

Many people turn to a therapist only when a major crisis such as death, divorce, or a suicide attempt takes place. Such events can shake them up so badly that they develop frightening symptoms, such as acute anxiety or depression. At other times the crisis is internal. A person may feel as if he or she is about to explode or is on the verge of a nervous breakdown, or he or she may be faced with scary thoughts about suicide or killing somebody else.

If you are in the midst of a crisis and have never seen a therapist, you may feel that you should not have put it off for so long, or you may think that it is too late now and there is nothing anyone can do but declare you hopelessly and helplessly lost forever. This is not true. Crises bring fear, pain, and risk, but also opportunities. When you realize you can't take it anymore, you are more likely to shift and change in profound ways.

There are less dramatic, yet good reasons to consult a therapist for one or a few sessions:

- OPENING UP WHERE IT IS SAFE: Sometimes you can't talk about a problem to an interested party. You may feel that if you tell the truth to a family member or friend, you will get into trouble. You may feel ashamed or guilty about something. You may want to see a therapist to keep your problem confidential, or you may want to hear a fresh and new perspective from an uninvolved party. In one or a few sessions you can feel that you are finally able to tell it all in an open and safe atmosphere.

A wise therapist will make you feel heard and may be able to validate feelings and thoughts that have been boiling in you for a long time. But watch out, don't let therapy be the only place where you can open up.

• SECOND OPINION: You are about to take an important step. You are contemplating your options. You may be thinking about breaking up a significant relationship, changing careers, getting married, or sending your child to a special school. You find yourself feeling ambivalent. Postmodern life often presents us with multiple viable choices. Most significant decisions in life are made with considerable ambivalence.

Whatever psychological issue you face and need a professional opinion on, keep in mind that you may get a wise opinion but not necessarily an objective or scientific opinion. Some psychotherapists claim they offer an objective opinion. That is a fallacy. All therapists are biased by their point of view and their personal experiences. A good professional opinion is one that helps you to make the decision that is best for you and that is based on your unique situation, personality, and intuition.

Getting into Therapy for the Wrong Reasons

Let's now turn to some of the mistaken, yet very common, reasons to seek therapy. Here is why you should *not* go to therapy. At times these may be not your explicit reasons but reflect your hidden agenda:

"I want to change what somebody else is doing."

Too often people try to change their children, their parents, their spouse, or an employee. When they fail, they turn to a therapist hoping she or he will fix what they could not. This approach is doomed to fail and can often make matters worse. For one thing, therapists can't change those who do not wish to change. Second, when a person perceives that someone is trying to change or help, he or she will take it as a "put-down" or power move. This will likely weaken the relationship or cause humiliation. Third, trying to force change reduces the chances that this person will ever seek therapy on his or her own and increases the chances of hurting his or her self-esteem. Trying to change another person rarely helps, but it is the best way to convince someone that therapy is a waste of time and money. My advice is don't initiate therapy in order to change somebody else. If somebody else's behavior bothers you, seek therapy only in order to change your reaction, feeling, or thinking about that behavior. You can change only your own behavior and reactions and hope that others will follow your example.

"I want to know who the crazy one is here."
When you are stuck in a conflict-ridden situation at home, work, or school or in a significant relationship, you may want a therapist to be the judge, to decide for you who is wrong and who is right or who is guilty and who is not. One of the most harmful ways to use a therapist is to put her or him in the judge's chair to pass moral judgments about other people.

Matching with the Right Therapist

A young psychiatrist meets an old psychiatrist on an elevator at the end of a long day. The young one looks bedraggled, disheveled, exhausted. The older one adjusts the knot of his tie on his uncreased shirt; he looks energetic, cheerful, and dapper. The young one asks him: "I don't get it. You're thirty years older than I am. How can you listen all day to people's pain and problems and come out looking like that?" The older one smiles and says, "Who listens?"

As a client, you want to avoid both the disheveled and the disinterested therapist. A therapist should see you only when the problem you presented is within his or her area of competence and he or she should feel the challenge and hope for changing it. The therapist should be able to engage fully while keeping a sense of perspective.

Therapy sessions can be totally wasted or even cause harm if conducted by the wrong therapist at the wrong time. Matching well in therapy does not mean you will fall in love with your therapist or have him or her agree with everything you say. You don't have to make your therapist into your mentor. When you worship somebody else, you diminish yourself. Therapy is about helping *you* be the best healer and problem solver you can be. It is about restoring your self-respect, self-worth, and self-mastery. The wise therapist will provide an atmosphere where you feel comfortable enough to be yourself, to open up, and to tell your story in an accurate and meaningful way. You and the therapist can communicate on the same wavelength. She or he should be able to understand your point of view and validate your feelings. This will be followed by his or her ability to persuade you to change your attitude to a more productive and positive one.

Therapists who are rigid, distant, and self-righteous are to be avoided. Such therapists talk to you from a one-upmanship position. They emphasize notions of the authoritative account and the impersonal, expert view. They convey to you that their knowledge is unitary, global, and objective. They discourage or even prevent dialogue about different points of view. They deny their own ethical and moral biases by claiming to present you with the objective truth. The therapist who makes you feel stupid, crazy, or weak is the wrong therapist for you.

The good therapists are your expert partners. They learn from you. They encourage you to assist them in the quest for understanding. They value your insight and look for your feedback. They inquire about which of the ideas and developments that arise in the therapy are the ones you prefer. They welcome any question you may have about the session itself or the process of therapy, thus contributing to a context of accessibility and partnership.

Other Considerations

There are no clear, objective, or scientific criteria for what matters to you and makes you feel good about your choice. Here is a partial list of possible considerations that may provide further guidance in the choice of a therapist:

- A RECOMMENDATION: A person you trust, a friend who has been in therapy, a family member, or your personal physician could be a reliable source for a recommendation. When you make a choice in this way, keep in mind that whoever recommends this therapist may very well have a different personality and a different set of problems than you do.
- FEES: You may choose a therapist because she or he works where you don't have to pay. Such places could be your HMO, your EAP, or your local community mental health service. Talking to a private therapist is not cheap, and financial con-

siderations are a legitimate part of selecting a therapist. On the other hand, you may be impressed by fees. When you pay more you expect to get more for your money.

- MEDICINE: You may trust medications and "real doctors." In such a case consult your personal physician, who is likely to know psychiatrists in the community.
- POPULARITY: You may be impressed by how busy the therapist is. If she or he didn't have an opening for a few months and people are waiting for her or him, then she or he must be good. If you hear people talking, you may be impressed by the word that a certain therapist is really the best in the area.
- AGE: You may find yourself trusting older therapists with wisdom and experience or young ones who are up-to-date with the latest technologies and have modern ideas.
- GENDER: You may feel safer or more at ease with a therapist of the same sex. Others feel much more attracted to a therapist of the opposite sex.
- SETTING: You may be impressed by the setting. For example, you may prefer a clinic in a prestigious university.
- SPECIALITY: You may want an expert for your specific problem, especially if you have a particular diagnosis or label for your problem. If you define it as a family problem, you may seek a family therapist. If you define it as a sexual problem, you will look for a sex therapist, and so on.

Some of the considerations listed here may be quite important to you, some less so. What might appeal to one person will be the very characteristic that distracts or dismays another. The status of a psychiatrist may impress one person and evoke suspicion in the minds of others who may prefer a social worker instead.

You need not argue with your biases, just use them to your advantage. Your biases are part of your belief system. When you feel more relaxed with a woman (or have any other cue that strengthens your trust in the therapist's ability to help you), you will be the first to benefit from it. If you have your doubts, don't hesitate to ask more questions or to take more time to make the right choice. This is a very personal and important decision, and should be based on your judgment and biases, not mine or those of any other person. In the end, other practical matters such as your budget, your schedule, and the location of the therapist's office will play a role, too.

Don't compromise. You have already waited. You deserve what is best for you. What is best for you is a therapist and a place that enhances your hope, positive expectations, and sense of trust. If, by the end of the first session, you have no sense of connectedness, and by the end of the third session you have made no progress, in all likelihood you either are seeing the wrong therapist or the timing is wrong.

It may be helpful to ask some questions during the initial phone contact. Ask:

- What kind of experience have you had with problems like the one I just described? Have you helped people in my situation?
- How confident are you about solving a problem like mine? What is your rate of success with problems like mine?
- I understand each case is unique. Yet, on the average, how long would you expect it to take? How often would you want to see me?
- Do you have one or a few preferred methods of psychotherapy? Can you briefly tell me about your preferred method for a problem like mine?

- What is your fee, schedule, and available time to see me? Can you be flexible about it?
- Do you prefer open-ended or time-limited therapy?

Make sure to specify your limitations or preference regarding schedule and fee. If you are interested in making therapy as brief as possible, say so directly. If the therapist you call prides herself or himself on open-ended therapy, you should know it prior to the first session. Many therapists use a sliding scale. For example, you can tell your therapist what your budget is for the entire treatment and ask whether or not he or she can work with you within it.

The key to therapy success is in the particular "chemistry" established when two people meet together. You may want to save some of the above questions for after you meet the therapist for the first time. You may even request a trial session, for no fee or a small fee, where you will be able to gather more face-to-face information. Recently, a former and very grateful client of mine referred her best friend to me. My former client knew me well, since I had helped her and her family through some very difficult times, including the death of both her parents. The friend was from a similar socioeconomic group and the presented problems were similar. Yet we never were able to get therapy off the ground. The chemistry was not right.

The best sessions are when a therapist helps you realize and unmask what you already know deep down about your possibilities and potential. You may say at the end of such a session to the therapist: "You strengthen my intuition" or "I knew somehow that this is what I need to do. Now, with your opinion backing me up, I feel more strongly that I not only need to do it, but I also want to and can do it." In other words, the wise therapist will translate your inner knowledge or feeling into a language of possibilities for action. You may know something and yet be unable to act on it. You may think something, and yet not quite feel it (or vice versa).

How to Evaluate a Therapist

How do you find a competent, trustworthy, and helpful therapist? The best way is to evaluate her or him as well as your own feelings after the first conversation you have on the phone or face-to-face. Selecting the right therapist is not a science, and in the end you will need to go by your gut feelings and intuition. First impressions are powerful and important and they can predict much of what is going to follow. Often, when I listen to or watch a tape of my first session with a client I am amazed at how much of the entire therapy was set in force by this one session.

Overall, two elements may be critical:

1. Coming out of the session and in the following days ask yourself whether your morale and sense of hope are improving as a result of the session. What other improvements have you noticed since the first session?

2. Consider the extent to which the therapist's response, proposed solution, or treatment plan made sense to you or at least was intriguing and challenging enough for you to think about.

Your First Impression of the Therapist

The following list may be helpful in assessing your first impressions. Answer yes or no.

My first impression of the therapist is that he or she is:

	YES	NO
1. Understanding (empathetic)		
2. Trustworthy		
3. Honest (genuine)		
4. Communicating clearly (makes sense)		
5. Genuinely interested in me and my views		
6. Competent		
7. Caring and warm		
8. A good listener		
9. An expert in his or her field		
10. Friendly and seems to like me		
11. Attentive to my needs		
12. Gentle and nurturing		
13. Respectful of my pace, patient with me		
14. Wise, smart		

RESULTS: You may have selected a therapist on the basis of one or a few criteria that made all the difference in the world to you. If that is the case, that's fine. Otherwise, you can evaluate your therapist by the following criteria: If you answered yes ten or more times, you truly made an excellent choice. Seven or more yes answers indicate a good therapist. Five or more can make a solid therapist. If you answered no ten or more times, it's time to shop for another therapist or reexamine your expectations.

Self-Evaluation

The most important criterion for selecting a good therapist is not how you feel about the therapist, but rather how the meeting with him or her made you feel about yourself and your problem. This is a relative, not absolute, rating. Compare it with how you felt before you first called her or him. It may be better to assess it a few days or a week after the first session, so you can better assess what filtered in and seemed to take hold. Don't look for radical changes. Small yet noticeable positive change is plenty.

When I compare it with how I was when deciding to call the therapist, I'm now more:

	YES	NO
1. Confident		
2. Clear-minded		
3. Hopeful		
4. Safe		
5. Faithful		
6. Validated and understood		
7. In control		
8. Changed (in my view or perspective of the problem)		
9. Kind toward and accepting of myself		

RESULTS: Again, a couple of these may eclipse the others in importance, and you can base your evaluation on those specific, highly-valued criteria. Here is a quantitative scale to use if all the criteria are of equal importance:

If you can answer yes to seven or more of the items, you can consider yourself not only lucky but also a very resourceful client who made a good choice of a therapist, with excellent timing. If you answered yes in four to seven of the items you can be satisfied with the progress you have made so far. If you answered no to more than five items, in particular items 3, 6, and

8, you need to reevaluate your relationship with the therapist. If you are hopeful and trust the therapist, let her or him know about your feelings. Otherwise, remember that a therapeutic relationship involves a special chemistry, and at times requires more than one trial before you find the right match. The briefer the therapy the more you want to concentrate on attaining your goal and less on your therapist's personality.

Making the Most of Every Session

Ongoing therapy can quickly become a routine activity you do every week. For some it may become a habit or even feel like a necessity of everyday life like eating and sleeping. When you are treated in classical psychoanalysis you may see your analyst up to five times a week. I remember the years when my friends and I would often use the phrases: "My therapist said . . ." or "You know, I should bring it up in my next session" in many of our daily conversations. We were like a little cult of psychotherapy addicts. One friend always held us back with his inability to choose a movie or restaurant. A standard joke was that he should first ask his therapist and then the therapist would ask him, as therapists often do, "What do *you* think, Mark?"

Another friend went daily to classical analysis as part of his training to become an analyst. He often called me frantically to ask if I could "lend him a dream." The poor guy was unable to recall a new dream every night, but as an analyst candidate he wanted to please his therapist with a new dream every session.

Therapists often forget to make each and every session count, because they don't pay for it and have many other patients to think about. It is your job, as a client, to make sure you get your money's worth and to make the therapist obsolete as soon as you can. Many therapists will resist your ending the treatment, especially if you have been a good, paying client.

Here are a few tips on how to make each and every session count whether you are in long-term or short-term therapy:

- NEVER UNDERESTIMATE YOUR CAPACITY FOR HEALTH, WELL-BEING, AND RESILIENCE. At any given moment you are likely to be attracted by the bad and dramatic news of the week and to ignore the ordinary and optimistic "good news." Keep reminding yourself that you are alive and constantly evolving and changing. When you begin to think, "I'm not good enough," remind yourself that this is only a thought and your thought can be changed any time. Now is usually the best time to change. After you have finished telling your therapist how difficult your life is, go back to yourself and take charge.

- DON'T JUDGE, CENSOR, OR BLOCK YOUR "GUT FEELINGS." Therapy is one of the best places to experience the responsible expression of all emotions. Emotions are a form of knowing. Our rationale may be more sophisticated and correct, but ignoring our emotions has a tricky way of destroying everything at once.

- TAKE IT ONE STEP AT A TIME. You may get discouraged because old habits and feelings keep resurfacing and interfering with the "new self." They do not! They are only securing the process of change so your development will be a true and lasting one. If you keep hoping that therapy will make you "happy ever after" or self-loving every minute of the day, I can guarantee you will need to stay in therapy forever, only to find out that therapy never gave you a shield from all bad feelings and events.

- YOU ARE THE PRIMARY AGENT OF CHOICE, CHANGE, AND ACTION IN YOUR THERAPY. Your choices and actions are going to make therapy work. Most of what the therapist does (when she or he is a good one) is be there, while not standing in your way. The late psychiatrist Eric Berne, who developed TA (transactional analysis) therapy well recognized this: "A patient has a built-in drive to health, mental as well as physical. His mental and emotional development has been obstructed, and the therapist has only to remove the obstructions for the patient to grow naturally in his own direction. The therapist does not cure anyone, he only treats him to the best of his ability, being careful not to injure, and waiting for nature to take its healing course."

- Compassion, Forgiveness, and Love Are Your Best Allies in Therapy and Life. At any minute you can direct them toward yourself or others. When you suffer from a problem, you probably need to restore one or all of these three natural therapeutic elements.

- Self-Caring Does Not Exclude Care for Others. It usually means mutually supporting one another. When you are in therapy you should not treat it as a vacation from your social responsibilities. Helping those who need it and appreciate it is one of the most rewarding activities. Your ability to exchange help and being helped is one of the most essential balances in life.

- Know When to Stop. If you feel you've had enough for now, stop therapy while you are ahead. All endings are also new beginnings and you may come back one day. Leave yourself an open door. Do not treat your gains or lessons from therapy as final or permanent. Happiness and a meaningful life do not lie comfortably nested within any model, scripture, or psychological theory. Such states of mind must be endlessly and individually re-created in our lived struggles and triumphs.

- If It Works—Don't Fix It. Change is not always in your best interest. Stability and continuity are useful and necessary elements in providing some coherence in chaotic lives. Do not try to analyze and "therapize" everything and everyone in your life. You may feel inclined to do that once you have tasted therapy. Beware: You'll run into two problems. First, you may end up talking about life instead of, or more than, simply living it. Second, you may end up using therapy as a way of feeling more insightful and clearer than your friends or peers and sooner or later they will resent that.

In summary, the right therapist at the right time will provide an atmosphere where you feel comfortable enough to be yourself, open up, and shift into a problem-solving, hopeful mode. You are not alone. Change is underway. You and the therapist can communicate on the same wavelength. He or she understands your point and is able to validate your feelings. The wise therapist will first help you to differentiate between attainable and unattainable goals, between soluble and insoluble problems. Once you focus on a problem, together you will select the solutions that best match your abilities and readiness.

Therapy in a New Key: Psychohealth, Solution, and Partnership

This chapter summarizes the three key concepts that govern the new thinking about psychotherapy: psychohealth, solution, and partnership. These concepts represent an alternative to the traditional model in psychiatry and psychotherapy: psychohealth replacing psychopathology, solutions replacing problems, and partnership replacing patronization, domination, and hierarchy. The ultimate test in any therapy is whether the therapeutic experience can be transferred to everyday life and the relationships in a client's life. I believe this can happen more quickly by emphasizing strengths and solutions.

I owe the shift in my attitude about psychological help to my clients. They showed me that those times when I felt that I had failed them and that they were "bad patients" were times when they really improved, took charge, and solved their problems in the most effective way—now and on their own. As a therapist, once I changed my frame of mind, I came to see therapy in a new light. I changed my practice. Once I was able to expect change, my clients changed rapidly. I started to meet people, not psychiatric cases. I searched for capabilities, not deficiencies. I set goals together with my clients rather than handing down their verdict, the diagnosis. I listened where I used to lecture. I learned where I used to teach.

Focusing on Capabilities and Hope

I was often asked how I could listen all day long to people's troubles, pains, and failures. With hindsight I realized how hard it was. It was difficult to hear people talking about their pains, failures, and troubled lives as long as it was a way of maintaining their self-pity and their image of themselves as victims and patients. My work as a listener and a therapist became exciting once I was able to see that clients are capable of growth and change in a matter of just a few weeks or even within the first hour.

By using the language of psychohealth, therapists and clients refocus their interest on the human potential and on the immense capability of each individual to learn and change. Psychohealth explores present capabilities, strengths, and willingness to learn and change. Psychohealth is part of the effort to feel more competent and content with life. Therapists who focus on psychohealth respect life and the innate capacity of people to heal themselves and solve their problems. They act with compassion and sensitivity.

People go to doctors and therapists out of a combination of hope and fear that something specific and diagnosable may be wrong and with hopes that what is wrong can be set right. What the therapist has, and most Western doctors don't have, is time to talk and to listen. Most physicians will offer their patients five to fifteen minutes, while the average therapist will allocate fifty to sixty minutes per session. The wise therapist is aware that when the patient talks about his or her life and problems, the talking itself can lessen the patient's anxiety. To facilitate the development of psychohealth, the therapist respects the desire and ability of patients to unburden themselves of their fears and self-doubts. In the first part of the session, the attentive and compassionate listening of the therapist helps to establish that the aim of the therapeutic encounter is to solve the problem and reduce the pain. The therapist helps the patient to recognize her or his abilities as well as the obstacles that caused pain, conflicts or dilemmas. Next, the psychohealth therapist will explore with the patient the areas that can strengthen the patient's physical and mental immune system—the natural system that defends us from illnesses.

The late Norman Cousins in his final book, *Head First: The Biology of Hope,* noted that the immune system, like therapy: "is a mirror to life, responding to its joy and anguish, its exuberance and boredom, its laughter and tears, its excitement and depression, its problems and prospects. Scarcely anything that enters the mind doesn't find its way into the workings of the body. Indeed, the connection between what we think and how we feel is perhaps the most dramatic documentation of the fact that mind and body are not separate entities but part of a fully integrated system."

Psychohealth treats a person as a whole, fully integrated system. When the psychohealth therapists search for their clients' hope and faith and not their pain and despair they count on the immense capabilities of body-mind as an integrated system. This hope is sound and reliable. I often cite Franz Ingelfinger, the former editor of *The New England Journal of Medicine.* In his farewell article he reminded physicians that 85 percent of human illnesses are within the reach of the body's own healing system and therefore require no medication or other medical intervention. All therapists and patients need to be constantly reminded that most of the people who suffer from psychological problems and mental disorders can solve the problems with their own problem-solving mechanisms, healing systems, and human support. Therapy and health care should enable the patient to access those elements.

Mobilizing the mental and physical immune system helps the body as well as the mind. Theodore Melnechuk, of the University of California Medical School in San Diego, reviewed extensive scientific evidence (including 530 references) regarding the influence of the psyche and the nervous and endocrine systems on bodily repair systems. One of the conclusions of this review is that positive emotions are associated with improved wound healing. Melnechuk further suggests that these emotions alter production of hormones, neurotransmitters, and opiates that influence the various steps in the healing process. On the other hand, distress has been shown to damage DNA (genetic) repair. (The review by T. Melnechuk is published in *Emotions and Psychopathology*, edited by M. Clynes and J. Panksepp, 1988.)

The Healing Power of Fear and Hope

Let's say you come to see the therapist because something is happening that you don't know how to deal with. The wise therapist will offer you hope and reassurance. In this way she or he puts the human spirit to work: The therapist helps you to confront a new challenge and summon your strength and resources.

Wise therapists will never minimize the seriousness of your problem; they will present it as a challenge that calls for the best that both therapist and patient have to offer. The psychohealth therapist serves in the same way as a midwife assists during birth—as a facilitator who helps you maximize your potential. The psychohealth therapist knows that freedom from depression and high stress as well as the strong will to be back in charge of your life is a vital factor in overcoming most serious troubles. Some problems cannot be solved, but they can be survived or outgrown. My work has taught me that the ability of human beings to tolerate stress is incontestably finite. Most of my patients face daily stresses and adversities I can't even imagine surviving for one day. When you have no choice, you find one from within. Viktor Frankl, founder of logotherapy and author of *Man's Search for Meaning,* describing the Holocaust survivors of the Nazi death camps, wrote that everything can be taken from a person but one thing: the last of human freedoms—to choose one's attitude in any given set of circumstances, to choose one's own way.

When you go to meet a therapist, be prepared to explore your positive emotions—joy, laughter, exuberance, hope—not just your negative emotions—depression, anxiety, helplessness. Be prepared to discuss your abilities and not just your disabilities, your strengths and not just your weaknesses. You may be wondering how you can do this when faced with a grave condition or serious illness.

Consider AIDS patients as an example. Dr. George Solomon of the UCLA School of Medicine studied a group of AIDS patients and found that when patients' needs were given attention, and when patients took an active role in their own health maintenance, both doctors and patients maintained positive attitudes and emotional fortitude. All of these factors were related to relatively good immune measures and compensatory increases in some categories of immune cells. Such AIDS patients enjoyed a relatively better quality of life in the course of their illness and lived far longer than expected.

The therapist, in my view, should be thought of as a trusted partner or as an expert in solutions and psychohealth. And that view will be associated with what all competent therapists and healers do: bolster a client's hope, morale, and faith. This is not a new model. This is an old truth coming alive again in the postmodern era. The Swiss physician Paracelsus wrote more than four hundred years ago: "Faith in the gods cure one, faith in little pills another, hypnotic suggestion a third, faith in a plain common doctor a fourth. . . . Faith in us, faith in our drugs and methods, is the great stock in trade of the profession." Imagine how you would feel if you underwent a physical exam and your doctor told you as he or she checked you: "That's a good strong heart you've got there; your kidneys are behaving like perfect little gentlemen; all in all, these tests rule out the possibility of any progressive active disease process anywhere." This approach is what Dr. Gilbert Day in his article published in the British medical journal *Lancet* identified as the therapeutic physical exam. One does not need to be in perfect health to hear such feedback from a doctor.

Dr. Oliver Sacks, a neurologist, reports of an extensive examination on one of his patients. The man suffered from a rare form of brain damage; his ability to think abstractly was intact but his ability to recognize concrete items was severely damaged. As a result, he made funny mistakes such as patting the top of parking meters, taking them to be the heads of children. His odd mistakes did not interfere with his career as a distinguished musician, which he carried on with success and joy. At the conclusion of two days of extensive examination, the patient turned to Dr. Sacks and asked: "Well, Dr. Sacks, you find me an interesting case, I perceive. Can you tell me what you found wrong with me?"

Sacks replied: "I cannot tell you what I find wrong, but I will say what I find right. You are a wonderful musician and music is your life. What I would prescribe in a case such as yours is a life which consists entirely of music. Music has been the center, now make it the whole of your life." Dr. Sacks diagnoses abilities, not pathology. He emphasizes what the patient has and can enjoy more of, instead of reporting what's wrong.

Feelings Revisited

To illustrate the meaning of the shift from pathology to health-based language, let's examine the subject of feelings in psychotherapy. Feelings are considered the heavyweight subject in psychotherapy, and emotional problems are the cornerstone of long-term therapy. The traditional view is that emotions are often hidden in our unconscious and can't be accessed due to defense mechanisms like denial and intellectualization. Therefore a delicate and lengthy process is required to uncover emotions. Let's view, for a moment, our ability to feel. I love only what I know to love. I can't love what I don't know to love. If I improve my ability, I will start to experience pleasure and love. It requires certain cognitive training and practice before we can start to enjoy these emotional abilities.

You may go to therapy in order to rehash how you feel about events in your past. You are likely to focus on your bad feelings about areas where you are incompetent. The psychohealth therapist will redirect you by identifying, improving, and focusing on your ability, to help you achieve effective and rapid emotional change. A shift in your feeling can occur in one session (or a few) as soon as you start to focus on your positive feelings (laughter, hope, love) and practice that focus, for example by self-affirmations, or celebrating pleasure and optimism. If you and your therapist are interested in exploring your helpless, paranoid, or anxious feelings, these are what will come to the center stage of therapy. The more you talk about your bad feelings, the more real and central they will become in your life.

Emotions are not buried inside. Everyone has thoughts and emotions because they participate and interact with other people. Certain people, events, and activities can make you feel alive, witty, and quite happy almost at once. Others may make you feel dull, stupid, and helpless. The meaning you give to your feelings is the result of the way you interact with others. Help your therapist by discussing with him or her topics like optimism, humor, purpose, and hedonism, and you will see how emotions can change quite rapidly simply by paying attention and practicing them. When therapy focuses on learning and practicing these feelings as much as it presently does on anger, frustration, anxiety, and depression, we are more likely to use therapy briefly in order to develop our skills in paying attention, expressing, and interacting with positive emotions. We don't need to uncover all our sadness in order to experience happiness. We don't need to discuss hate in order to develop love. We don't need to talk about problems in order to find viable solutions. We only need to pay more attention to and practice more of what we wish to accomplish.

Talking Solutions Instead of Problems

One of the jobs of a useful therapist is to help shift a client from problem talk to solution talk—to identify viable solutions available in the client's repertoire and present them in a form that allows them to be practiced. Focusing on solutions is a natural element in the psychohealth approach, and one that is taking hold among many therapists. I'll only summarize here what was researched and written about extensively by Steve de Shazer, Insoo Berg, and Scott Miller from the Brief Therapy Center in Milwaukee, Wisconsin; William O'Hanlon of The Hudson Center for Brief Therapy in Omaha, Nebraska; and Michele Weiner-Davis in Woodstock, Illinois.

The basic beliefs of the solutions therapist are:

1. Clients bring into therapy the resources that are necessary to resolve their complaints. Therapy helps them to find these resources within themselves.

2. Personal change goes on continuously, with or without therapy.

3. The task of the therapist is to identify and amplify positive and useful changes and solutions.

4. A client can solve a problem without knowing its causes or the functions of its symptoms.

5. Small changes may be sufficient. Big or complex problems don't require big solutions. Solutions reverberate throughout the system and personality and can bring about changes in many other areas of functioning.

Here is a chart of the main differences between conventional and solutions therapy:

CONVENTIONAL THERAPY	SOLUTIONS THERAPY
Theory:	
Past-oriented	Present- and future-oriented
Length:	
Long-term	Short-term

Goal:

Emphasize depth, gain insight	Prioritize effectiveness and practicality
Identify and correct psychopathology	Identify and amplify change

Patients:

Resistant to change	Eager to gather resources necessary to resolve problems

Attitude:

Ambivalent about change	Personal change goes on continuously with or without therapy
Real change takes time	

Cause/Diagnosis:

Deep, underlying causes for symptoms	Resolving symptoms does not require knowing their causes or functions
Symptoms are functional	
Correct diagnosis is necessary for choosing correct treatment	There is no single correct diagnosis

Right from the start, solutions therapy focuses on what the client is already doing that works. It assumes that every complaint or problem has an exception which the client has overlooked or de-emphasized, as if the problem were always happening, when in fact, there are usually moments and periods when the problem does not exist.

Solutions-therapy intervention involves asking the client to continue doing the exception to the problem (maybe a bit more often than before). Thus, a previously unrecognized act of mental health becomes a recognizable and effective element. In other words, the therapist helps the client construct what he or she did differently into a consistent, noticeable norm rather than a dismissable exception.

Making the Exception into the Rule

Pat came to therapy in order to lose weight. "Let's face it. Thin is in," she said. "Being a working woman is hard enough out there. I simply can't afford to be fat, too." Looking for the exception to being fat, the therapist asked her when she had been able to lose enough weight so that she didn't see her physical size as a problem.

"I have tried every diet known to woman," she replied. "Drastic diets like injections and fasting got me to the weight I wanted, but I very quickly regained it."

"So you know how to lose weight. But you want to be able to keep it off," the therapist suggested.

"That's right!"

"Can you recall any time during your life when you felt your weight was just right over any extended period of time?"

"Well, when I was in college, I was more active and in much better shape."

When Pat came for therapy, she was 28 and still living at home, where her mother constantly harassed her about her weight. Pat was career-oriented but felt a lack of challenge and progress in her present job. The therapist began exploring with Pat various career options that required going back to school. The therapist's goal was to translate the "exception" (staying thin while being away from home, at college), into the "rule." This exception was linked to a subject that motivated her to advance in her career. The therapist suggested to Pat that when she felt really ready to advance in her career, she join a graduate program that allowed her to live on campus. He also suggested that when she get there, she start taking dancing and singing lessons again (activities she liked while in college). No specific diet was prescribed, as diets had only failed her in the past. A year later, Pat called to tell the therapist that she got so involved with graduate school, she didn't have time to obsess about food and diets. "I lost weight and I've kept it off for the past six months. To tell you the truth, I did nothing special. It was completely natural."

Some clients need therapy to remind them of what they have done that is positive and help them appreciate and value that worthwhile behavior. Differences and changes occur all the time, but if they are not recognized, they have no long-term effect. Once a therapist helps a client to recognize a useful difference, then the client can put it to work. The process of achieving the goal can take longer than the therapy itself. In Pat's case, SST was used to find the appropriate solution and start a process which Pat continued on her own. (This case is based on two similar cases, one treated by Dr. Robert Rosenbaum at Kaiser Medical Center in Hayward, California, and the other by Moshe Talmon in Israel. Both therapies lasted a single session.)

The Partnership Therapist

We are part of a community of people. Family, friends, and support groups all can be helpful in combatting helplessness and loneliness. Strong support from family and friends can help restore emotional equilibrium. These people often serve as "co-therapists." I see both formal therapy and informal therapeutic experiences as forms of partnership.

Here is a chart of the main differences between the conventional hierarchical model and the partnership model:

HIERARCHICAL	PARTNERSHIP
Therapist is in charge	Client and therapist are partners
Trust the therapist and follow his or her orders	Follow the wisdom of mind and intuition
Power over patient	Power with client
Indoctrination	Education
Control	Nurture
Ranking	Linking
Patronizing	Exchanging, sharing

Therapy is a form of communication based on mutual respect. The power of the therapeutic relationship lies in the alliance between two partners: client and therapist. Power in the partnership is not control and domination over others, but the power to create for oneself and others a better way of being and relating. The therapy of the partnership model is designed to help reclaim that power and rejoin a specific community of people.

In the partnership model, the therapist inspires rather than commands. She or he brings forth the best in the client, rather than cowing him or her into submission. She or he elicits creativity and trust rather than obedience and fear. The therapist's first job is to hear the client. The therapist does not have to like or agree with what you, as a client, have to say. But he or she has to learn from your knowledge of yourself, your life, and your worldview.

Partnership therapy helps to change fear-based behavior into trust-based behavior by forming a therapeutic, human alliance.

For example, when you suffer physical pain, you do not totally defer to external medical advice. Instead your first step is to uncover the knowledge and healing power that lies in the partnering of your mind and body. Instead of ignoring or getting irritated with pain, you can pay attention to changes that occur and modify actions on the basis of these changes. You may change your eating or sleeping patterns or simply allow time for rest and relaxation.

The same can be true for mental pain. For example, say your problem is that your children are out of control. You have tried endlessly and unsuccessfully to order them around. Solving the prob-lem in a partnership way would be to take more time with your family to work out shared, not ordered, responsibilities. You explain things to your kids and enlist their cooperation, not obedience.

In summary, partnership may work for the therapist/client relationship as well as in friendships, self-help groups, and coping with ongoing life problems. A good example is work-related problems. Ron lost his job as a result of a massive layoff in the company where he had worked for twenty years. For the first time in his life, he was out of work. His chances of finding another job seemed slim. He was sinking into anxiety and deep depression, and at first found comfort only in drinking beer with his fellow unemployed. In our first (and only) session, Ron agreed to my suggestion that he join a group of his former co-workers who had invited him to supportive and brainstorming meetings for people seeking new jobs. In addition, Ron's wife encouraged him to finish a long-awaited remodeling job in the house. She also arranged to get the extended family together more often. All of this kept Ron more active, and feeling hopeful and supported. I made two brief follow-up phone calls and learned that he needed no further therapy.

John was feeling increasingly anxious over the prospect of layoffs at his company. He first talked it over with a trusted co-worker, realizing his friend felt the same way. Their talk gave him an immediate sense of relief. "He understood me since he went through the same experience." At the end of their long discussion, they were both joking about "how misery likes company" and how little they can accomplish by worrying about the future of their company and the U.S. economy. John decided to start using a self-hypnosis tape he had purchased but never used. His friend decided to start professional training in a new line of work for possible relocation. Both were viable solutions that decreased anxiety and increased their sense of self-control.

To transform a crisis into an opportunity, or a deadlocked conflict into alternatives and choices, a therapist can help shift a client's perspective from a combative posture of attacking or defending, to the calmer posture of a participant-observer who tries to find access to new territories, points of view, and experiences.

Daniel, for example, was miserable in his marriage and hopeless about its future. He was contemplating divorce. He had three young children whom he loved dearly, and the idea of not seeing them every day petrified him. The recent economic recession and his family's financial situation made the prospect of maintaining two households very difficult to even consider. Daniel felt stuck when he consulted me.

I helped him see that the options were not limited to staying married or getting divorced, both of which looked like losing propositions. I suggested instead that he determine how he would like to raise his kids and be a proud father to them. I said that this was a goal he wanted and could attain, whether he was married or divorced.

"If I understood you correctly," I said, "you have no intention of divorcing your kids or ignoring the fact that they need both a father and a mother, regardless of your marital status." He readily agreed. I asked him to focus on what works for him regardless of his ultimate decision. Subsequently, he was able to shift from a losing dilemma between miserable marriage and traumatic divorce to a winning option in pursuit of his goal to be a responsible and warm father, whether he ultimately decides to divorce or not.

Future Therapy and Therapist

The partnership model is not limited to therapy with individuals, couples, or families. It is also useful in group therapy and in the various self-help programs. The basic premise of those programs is that through partnership—through sharing of feelings, ideas, mutual respect, and, above all, mutual empowerment—people can heal themselves. Partnership is an ongoing, accessible process. Students can become active partners in their schools, workers in their workplace, citizens in their government, and patients in their healing process.

Going to see a therapist once, or a few times, should not be viewed as a "once and for all" proposition. The therapist is there, in the community, at all times and a client can revisit him or her whenever necessary. The decision to be in therapy does not have to be an either/or decision. The services of therapy can be used effectively by utilizing them intermittently.

In summary, instead of the traditional psychological focus on explanations, problems, and pathology, the alternative model focuses on solutions, competence, and capabilities. The tradition in psychiatry, clinical psychology, and conventional psycho-therapy is to follow the medical model. In this model, the first job of a therapist is to diagnose a psychopathology or a mental illness—to point out what's wrong and why. In contrast, I suggest that the therapist's first job is to identify and focus on psycho-health and present to the client the challenge of utilizing it to combat the problem. Psychohealth explores the internal and external mechanisms for warding off physical illness and mental disorders or for coping with them if they recur. It teaches how hope, laughter, and human partnership strengthen the physical and mental immune system. It suggests that people view the signs of problems and pains as challenges to change, rather than indications of illnesses.

From Dilemma to Choice: Account of a Session

Emma, a 58-year-old woman, came to see me because she felt torn. She faced a dilemma that caused her stress, confusion, and feelings of helplessness. Segments from the single-session consultation with her are presented here word-for-word to illustrate how therapy in a new key is conducted, focusing on strength, solutions, and partnership. The following conversation happened at our first and only meeting.

Moshe: What is it that you would like to accomplish today?
Emma: The best thing for me would be to tell you my problems and have you tell me: Do this and that and everything will be all right. (She smiles, seeing the humor in it.)
Moshe: So, you want me to decide for you and tell you what you should do?
Emma: Not really. I guess I want to clarify a few things, gain some perspective and have a clearer picture of what's going on.

Moshe: O.K. Tell me in your own words, what's going on?

Emma: I'm married and our marriage has been a solid one for the past thirty-seven years! We raised four kids, two of whom are married already. My younger son and daughter are now in college. I was a nurse, and a teacher in nursing school, and I liked my work. We have lived on the East Coast all our lives.

Two years ago my husband started talking about going to Europe on a sabbatical. He got so excited that he arranged to work in a hospital in Germany, and actually got up one day, packed his bags, and left! We started to talk on the phone and he put a lot of pressure on me to leave everything and join him in Germany.

We have always been a very close family. My son still came home on weekends, and my girl was finishing high school at that time, almost two years ago. I said to my husband, "I am not ready to leave everything and just go." He started to pressure me. "It'll be wonderful," he said. But I did not want to leave my work, leave my kids.

Well, after my daughter graduated, I went to Germany for two months, and he has actually forced me to stay with him since then.

Moshe: What do you mean "forced" you?

Emma: I have a husband, I have responsibilities to him too, I can't live just for the sake of my kids. So, I took one year's leave from my work. I have had a very hard time, not speaking the language, missing my kids and my grand-children, being lonely. I started to fly back and forth, spending three months in the U.S. and three months in Germany. This is the second year I've been going back and forth. And I haven't stopped feeling torn apart.

I gave up my work, I left my family, my kids, all my friends. Of course I have my husband, I love him, I am happy to be with him, we have a wonderful time together and good sex. I am not used to this. I am a simple woman. I was happy with what I was doing. Now, I get up in the morning and say to myself, "tomorrow I am packing my suitcase, going back home." Then, the next day, I say—"Oh, I can't leave my husband alone, with all his work and pressure and everything!" And he keeps saying, "Stay with me."

Every day I change my mind, and I feel awful inside.

A conventional therapist, hearing such a story, would explore the history and roots of the problem. Is Emma an overinvolved mother or is she too dependent on her husband? Is her husband domineering, chauvinistic, selfish? And so on. Instead, I elected to focus on her strength: struggling with and surviving a difficult situation.

Moshe: That's a difficult dilemma! How on earth have you managed? What characteristics have allowed you to continue the day-to-day living?

Emma: I am a strong woman.

Moshe: I can sense that you are a strong woman. Is this strength something you inherited or did you develop it yourself? (Smiles.) What's your secret?

Emma: (Smiles as if she is revealing a secret.) I keep encouraging myself. I say, "Now you are here, have a good time, enjoy yourself." At the same time, I am looking forward to my next flight home. And when I am back home, I am so happy, with all the family! When Sunday comes and we all sit down together for brunch, I say, "Oh, my poor husband is alone now; I am having a great time with my children and grandchildren, and he must be so lonely." When I am in Germany I am just with him. I gave up my work. My boss said I can come back no later than two years from now. I miss my job. I am not doing anything serious in Germany. What I am doing now is having a good time. But this is not enough for me.

Moshe: So by going back and forth you are trying to stay loyal to your marriage and your husband, while being a good mom to your kids back home.

Emma: That's right.

The dilemma was clarified. Emma was caught between her loyalty to her husband and her attachment to her children and grandchildren, as well as the sense of home and the fuller life she had in the U.S.

When a person like Emma is overburdened and stressed out by conflicting responsibilities, I ask myself how she can broaden her support system. Could she trust others to carry some of the burden and responsibilities? Emma could not be a superwoman for all seasons in all places. I sensed that her heart went out to her younger children. So, I explored how they managed and whether she could learn to see them at this point as young adults.

I found out that her youngest daughter (whom she was most concerned about) was close to the extended family and had its support. I also learned from Emma that her son is aware of her conflict, accepts it, and leads his own life.

I began to look for ways to reframe the situation, so that Emma could live with it feeling less stress. Could she view herself as a good enough mother, being with her kids only part of the time?

Emma: When I'm with my kids, I'm doing a good job, I'm trying my best. Because I took a leave from my work, I have more time to spend with them, to go places, to just be together and have a good time.

Moshe: Looking at your options—from the very worst to the very best—can you tell me a bit about the options you're considering now?

Emma: I thought that at the end of the two years, I would go to my workplace to get my job back and say to my husband: "Listen, I spent two years with you, now I want to go back home." But then, the voice in the back of my mind still says I have to be with my husband, because he is lonely, he has no family. I mean, he finishes his work at four-thirty in the afternoon. He will be alone all evening.

Moshe: You are a very responsive and resourceful wife and mother. Have you thought of some other options?

Emma: The other option is to keep going back and forth.

Moshe: In a sense, you are creating with your body the bridge over the Atlantic Ocean between the two parts of your family.

When a person like Emma is caught between "a rock and a hard place" she needs to recognize the strengths and abilities she has already been using in order to cope. At the same time, I challenged her role as the one who sacrifices, in order to see if she might be willing to put the dilemma in her husband's court.

Moshe: You elected to come to this session by yourself. Is that because you feel that the decision is in your hands, and that you should make it on your own?

Emma: His position is clear: "Do what you want, but stay with me." He is not interested in changing the situation. He has left it up to me. I know that I'll be responsible for my decision; that I know.

Moshe: You are clearly a devoted wife and a devoted mother. The dilemma is that right now these two roles do not go hand in hand. Also, you have been married for thirty-seven years, and I hear from what you say that you would like to stay married.

Emma: Yes.

Moshe: And I've also heard you say that it takes a great toll on you. Do you feel it's your job to be the one who sacrifices, rather than your husband's? Do you feel that you have been selected to be in that role? After all, your husband made the choice to go to Germany! Let's imagine for a moment that you told him loud and clear: "This is what's right for me, it's right for me to have a job, it's right for me to be near the children. I took two years away from it all. But enough is enough. Now it's up to you. You'll decide what's right for you. O.K.?" How would you feel about taking such a position?

Emma: I'd feel that would be abandoning my husband. I feel that I must do everything perfectly: be a good mother, a good worker and a good wife. And I *know* that it cannot be done.

Moshe: It cannot be done. We cannot be perfect.

Emma: I cannot be perfect.

Emma insisted that she and her husband still had a great time together as a couple, even under these circumstances.

Moshe: Although you went through a difficult two years, there are a few things that I find remarkable.

One is that you didn't punish your husband for making you go to Germany. You did your best to make it a good time for the two of you as a couple. In fact, it's impressive and a tribute to you that you've found the enjoyment and pleasure that you have, in both places, given the stress you're under.

The second thing that strikes me is that your children are able to love and support you whether you are at home or away. And this is clearly a mutual feeling. They are saying in a sense: "We are doing O.K. It's difficult, very difficult, but we are doing O.K." And certainly you have found ways to devote time and love to them.

Emma agreed and we continued exploring the possibility of her settling down in the U.S. and going back to work.

Moshe: You're trying to keep your marriage together and you want to be a good wife to your husband, to spend more time with him alone. Do you think it's possible to reverse things? To spend a shorter but better quality time with him from now on, until he makes his decision?

Emma: I can. I know I can. When I am there this is what I do: I devote most of my time to him. I really spoil him. I give him a great time, and we are very happy. And he appreciates this. He has his work, which he loves, and he has a wife who loves him and does everything for him. So he doesn't need anything; he is happy.

Toward the conclusion of the session, I tried to give Emma a sense of hope and a renewed belief in her ability to make the right choices. I talked with her about what all of these struggles taught her about self-respect and what the next step would be in developing that respect. She replied that if she takes her efforts less for granted her husband will show more consideration and take her less for granted, too. I concluded the session by saying:

Moshe: You've done a remarkable job in facing what could be seen as an insoluble problem. I feel you have enough strength to keep doing it. But you now realize that there is a certain price which you may not be willing to pay. You want to go back to your job, and remain near your children, while maintaining your commitment to your marriage. I think that can be accomplished in two ways: One is using the ability you have now to give yourself and your husband a good time together. This is a commitment that you will maintain, wherever you reside. The second is that you should help your husband not take you for granted, in much the same way as you are not taking him for granted. When you are in the States (temporarily or permanently), you'll continue to maintain the quality of your marriage. If you stay in Germany (for however long you choose), you'll find ways to maintain the quality of your relationship with your grown-up children. In any case, you'll make sure your husband knows your position, appreciates you, and respects the choices you're going to make. He loves you, and you are a very capable woman who can convey a clear and strong message.

In a follow-up letter six months after the consultation Emma wrote to me:

"After our consultation I went back home several times in order to be with my kids. Time and time again I realized that they are grownups, having lives of their own and they don't need me in the same ways as they did before. My youngest daughter, whom I was most concerned about, is graduating from college next month and plans to take a trip overseas. My second youngest is now in Tokyo as part of an extended trip to the Far East. The two oldest ones are married with kids and are very busy with their careers and families. While visiting them I felt at times "out of work." Life is very dynamic and full of changes. I realized that in such times of flux it is important to spend more time with my husband. Time passes quickly, we are getting older and want to enjoy life and be with one another. My husband decided to come back to the States in one year; together we worked out a plan to gradually start the process of returning home. In three months we will start looking for an apartment in New York, not too far from our children and grandchildren. Before we return to the States permanently, we plan to take several trips in Europe. Now I am content with myself and happy with my decisions. I feel we made a good decision; the stress is relieved. I feel much better. Thank you for being there, for helping me to clarify my dilemma and work toward a good decision, which I believe satisfies all of us."

Self-Therapy

"I'm at my wit's end," said Judy when she first called me. "I'm totally overwhelmed, stressed out, and depressed."

After hearing a few more details, I said, "Before you come to see me I want you to think a little about how your life will be different once you don't need to come to see me anymore."

I gave her an appointment for ten days later. A day before the first session she called to say, "I think I don't need the session anymore."

"I'm curious. What has happened?" I asked.

"Well, I thought about what you asked me and found that what I really need to do is unload one of my too many responsibilities. I called the university to tell them that I'm quitting my teaching job. They were sorry to hear my decision, but accepted it. You see, the teaching job required constant reading of many students' papers. All are on the same subject and all have to be corrected late at night after a long day of work and parenting. I realized it was one of too many things I did. I already feel as if a burden has been lifted off my shoulders."

This chapter will focus on whether or not—and how—you can solve psychological problems on your own. When it comes to medical problems, most people have been educated to "call the doctor" if they're in pain or feel sick. With the great advances in technology and medicine, many people have come to expect life to be painless and perfectly comfortable. Only sometimes do they begin to feel that they have developed a dangerous dependency on their physicians and the marvelous technologies of painkillers, antibiotics, laser and plastic surgery, and so on.

Can you recall occasions when you felt much better by the time you arrived at the doctor's office? Can you recall picking up a full bottle of prescribed medication, only to find out that you didn't really need them anymore? People often forget that many problems and illnesses are states of mind, which can be resolved or cured without medical intervention, or they may be phases of minor illnesses that heal themselves with time.

I'm convinced that most people who go to therapy know the problem as well as the solution to it. Often, before they come to my office they have already made significant steps toward a solution.

Furthermore, after fifteen years of practicing psychotherapy and studying dozens of the most advanced therapeutic methods, I have come to believe that all effective therapies are basically self-therapies. The most powerful methods of therapy, such as hypnosis, biofeedback, and even psychoactive drugs, all work effectively only when they are combined with a patient's inner knowledge, will to live, and readiness to mobilize his or her internal and external resources. For example, every deep trance of hypnosis is not an act achieved by a talented hypnotist or brilliant magician. It is, in the end, a case of self-hypnosis. The suggestion and trance states are processes of self-hypnosis, which the hypnotist guides the patient through. Thus, even under a very deep trance, people have full control and knowledge of the situation. As a client, your experience is unique to you and only you can truly construct and decide upon its meanings. Expecting someone else to read your mind or understand it for you is like asking somebody else to breathe or drink for you.

Uncovering Pathways to Your Potential

Many people prefer to solve intimate and personal problems on their own. This approach is right as long as people follow up on their words with actions and really take care of the problem. Don't just say "I'll take care of it myself," as a way of putting it off or getting somebody off your back. You have the capacity to overcome the vast majority of your problems, diseases, and stresses either alone or with the help of others who care for you and yet won't charge a cent. Even though people turn to themselves or others again and again throughout life, most are not aware of their full potential for self-healing, although their bodies and minds are endowed with biological and psychological mechanisms that enable them to respond adaptively to an immense diversity of challenges. Because each person has a "hidden therapist," most pressures and stresses do not result in disease. People simply need to learn how to access it consciously, and hold on to it when they feel helpless.

The hidden therapist is your inner wisdom; it is the healer within that can cure self-limiting illnesses. Even when mental or medical disease does occur, your hidden therapist often brings about spontaneous recovery without the need for medical or psychiatric intervention. In this chapter you are invited to pay attention to and cultivate your blessings and good fortune: that is, your own force that protects you and fosters your mental and physical health, even under the most adverse conditions. In fact, you survive daily attacks by multiple agents of disease without even being aware of it. The reason is that your self-healing and immune system destroy those agents without causing you noticeable pain, fever or stress.

Your first job in self-therapy is to find a thread of hope and some sense of trust in yourself or the people around you. Trust that you and the natural force of life can bring about changes that are positive and desirable and will make a tangible, specific difference in your life.

If you just stand in front of the mirror and say a hundred times: "I trust myself. I'm hopeful," it may not be enough to turn things around. Telling yourself: "I'm happy. I'm fine," may feel like a bad joke. You can take it beyond trying to talk yourself out of the problem or cheer yourself up. Self-affirmation is recommended by most self-help books and cognitive therapists. It's a nice idea but is often not enough.

Self-therapy is therapy without a professional therapist. It is the natural process of change achieved by utilization of the self and others who care for you. Self-therapy evokes the hidden therapist in you and uses it actively in the search for better and more effective solutions. As Marilyn Ferguson puts it in *The Aquarian Conspiracy:* "The best anti-depressants are expression and action. That way our depression is not an end but a meaningful beginning."

When you try to solve your problem, choose a novel approach. You don't need to change your entire life. You may only need to achieve or allow a new balance. For example, if you have been doing too much thinking about your life, you may need to listen to the ideas of others. If you have been extremely busy for too long, you may need to take a break—do nothing for a while. In order to act in your own best interest you don't necessarily have to go very far or try very hard. Your body-mind and the world around you provide you with natural mechanisms that balance activity and rest, day and night, ups and downs. The problem-solving mechanisms are already well developed in your body-mind.

Most of the suggested exercises in this chapter are small and simple but can make a big difference. The basic principle in self-therapy is to do only what suits you and do only what you are ready to do right now. Take only the parts that are right for you. Let go of the rest. Moreover, feel free to create your own variations. If you wish, you can make notes in the margins of these pages. Add your ideas or highlight the things you wish to use. You are an active and indispensable partner in this process. I will present you with a series of potential solutions and simple exercises and you will adopt only those which are useful and feel right for you. They are based on my work with SST clients, many of whom started the process of change before they arrived at the first session. Self-therapy may save you from going to see a therapist or it may bring you to the first session with more confidence and a clearer goal in mind.

In any case, take it one step at a time and stop at any point. This may be your work/play book for as long as you wish. You can always come back and try something else at a later date. You do not have to complete all of the exercises in one sitting. They may start a process that will require a longer time to filter in and be tested by future challenges. You can use self-therapy instead of formal therapy, before you go to therapy, after you have terminated therapy, or even between sessions.

WHAT CAN BE ACCOMPLISHED IN SELF-THERAPY? These are some of the possibilities for what can occur using self-therapy:
- The letting go of your grievances instead of clinging to them.
- Freedom to take a lighter, more effective approach to "deadly serious" problems or to the feeling of being overwhelmed.
- An opening up of new possibilities, which will eventually allow you to reclaim your life and rejoin a community of people.
- The replacment of a sense of failure with a sense of success.
- The replacment of a sense of helplessness with a sense of self-mastery.
- Increased cooperation and decreased unproductive conflicts.

Changing Attitudes

Most psychological problems are a result of attitudes. You can always change your attitude, particularly if you realize how much trouble and pain that change can save you. Start by examining your attitude and exploring alternative ones. One of the most common thoughts people have when they are stuck is that they have no way out or that they have tried everything and nothing works. In order to get out of where you feel stuck, I suggest that while reading this chapter you try to consider any number of the following attitudes. Use only what fits your beliefs or the ones you wish to adopt now in order to enhance your problem-solving mechanisms. These are not the ten commandments, just a little food for thought.

- What happened to me in the past is over and done with and cannot be changed. What I can change is the perception and memory of my history and the meaning I construct around certain events.
- What governs my sense of self-worth and being "normal" is not the events themselves but the stories I (and others) construct about the events.
- Therapy is the process of reconstructing my memories, redefining my roles, reauthoring the story of my life.
- I may claim more control over my life by rewriting my story. (The translation of this idea to therapeutic work is further developed by Michael White and David Epston in *Narrative Means to Therapeutic Ends*.)
- The depression, guilt, anger, and other painful feelings I may go through are mostly the product of my memory and thoughts about the past.
- Every problem, every crisis, carries with it the seed of its solution. Pain and suffering are symptoms of my potential health. I'll never ignore the signals of my body. They guide my changes.
- Yesterday is gone and tomorrow isn't here yet. The time to change my actions, feelings, or thoughts is at the present moment.
- There is more than one right way to solve a problem.
- I'll never know until I try. If something does not work, I can always try something else.
- No solution works for everybody all the time. Yet, if it has worked once, it may work again.
- I welcome the unexpected.
- Failures are only necessary lessons.

- Life is an adventure in forgiveness. I forgive myself and those who failed me. I'll do it over and over again.
- Nobody is perfect. The fact that there is always room for improvement does not mean I'm thoroughly inept or without skills.
- Fun and good things will come my way, but I can't expect them to be foremost in life all the time.
- I'm bound to take rides uphill and downhill and each is necessary in order to appreciate the other.

Notice All That You Wish Would Keep Happening

If you are a born optimist you may skip this exercise. For the next few days I want you to note *everything* that happens to you that you would like to have keep happening in the future. Notice big and small events, important and unimportant—anything that you perceive with one of your five senses and wish to have keep happening. For example, note if somebody smiles at you or if you hear a punch line that makes you laugh, you see a sight you think is beautiful, you smell a scent that evokes pleasure, you witness an act by yourself or your loved ones that makes you proud, you use a capability or strength and it is appreciated.

It may sound like a very simple and easy task. It's easier said than done. Your mind plays many tricks to test your level of determination. People often give immediate attention to catastrophes and bad events. They are likely to be glued to the TV when wars, earthquakes, and riots are being shown. They are much less likely to rush and see the first day of spring or the sight of flowers opening up. People are apt to pay attention to the things they don't have or don't like about themselves. Negative feelings occupy a fearsome amount of space in the mind, blocking other perceptions, prospects, or pleasures.

Do not get discouraged. When you find your attention getting directed to bad events or negative thoughts, simply acknowledge the interference and let it go. Shift back to your exercise. You will find yourself going back and forth. That is okay. Return to paying close attention to your blessings—small yet significant good fortunes. Start with very small events such as a greeting or smile from a stranger or an unexpected phone call from a person who cares.

When people feel depressed or anxious, they can get out of it by paying close attention to the fact that their feelings are never constant. Certain people, times, and places may evoke different feelings, different energy. Those feelings may not last all day, nor feel very strong or significant. All you should do is notice that they are making a difference and welcome them. Do not try to hold on to them or make them constant. Just make a mental or written note of their presence.

You can't control all that happens in your world, but you can shift your attention from one part of the experience to the other. You can shift your thoughts and feelings or the actions you take. For example, if it is a very cold winter day you may notice how much you hate it when it is so cold and imagine other, hot climates where you're sure you'd be happier. Or, you may elect to dress very warmly and go watch children playing in the snow, or you may skip your plan for the day and get under the warmest blanket in the house to read a book or watch a movie. Most of life's healthy pleasures cost nothing: a belly laugh, an act of love, paying attention to the wonders and beauty of nature's sights, smells, and sounds.

Just notice it!

Telling Your Story

The effects of confronting a problem openly in an environment free of judgment and fear can be truly remarkable. Tell the story of your most traumatic experience or an event that hurt you significantly. This exercise is useful only if your problem is connected (in your mind) to a secret or traumatic event in your past, and no matter how hard you try to forget, ignore, and tuck away the problem, intrusive thoughts, anxiety, or sleep problems bother you. Do not pick a story you have already told and retold a thousand times.

Tell your story as it is and in full. Tell it from beginning to end. Use no external or internal censor or editor. As you tell your story you may experience strong feelings. Notice them and describe them as you move along, but remember to go back to your story. This is not self-analysis. Do not analyze your story or draw conclusions from it. Tell it as you remember it without skipping anything, no matter how minor or stupid it may sound to you.

You may find it easier to write it down. You can do this on a clean piece of paper, in front of a computer screen, or in your secret diary. Some might prefer to tell it out loud. You can use a large mirror to tell it to yourself looking straight into your own eyes. This approach can be very powerful. A less intense, yet helpful method is to use a tape recorder (if you do it by yourself) or telephone if you wish to tell it to somebody else.

Whatever way you select, make sure to do it in a comfortable and familiar setting. Sit or lie down comfortably and make sure there will be no interruptions (disconnect the phone, do not be anxious about your next appointment). Use the mode of communication that is most natural and least restrictive for you. There is no proper way of doing it other than the one in which you feel most natural and comfortable.

You may do it on your own if you are accustomed to writing essays, personal letters, or diary entries. Otherwise, you may tell it to a trusted friend. We each have our own preference. I myself prefer to share my fun and successful experiences with others, but find that I need to be alone, in my own corner, when I "lick my wounds," feel depressed, or stuck. If you wish to do it on your own, writing your story down may be a first step before sharing it with another person (or just for keeping your own record). You don't have to tell it to anybody or confront the person who may have abused or hurt you. Opening up to yourself or a trusted friend is good enough.

If you do wish to tell somebody, pay attention to the process of choosing the right person at the right time. For example, Kim, who was molested by her father, wanted to confront him. Yet, when she did so he denied the whole story and worse yet, he was under the influence of alcohol during the meeting. The whole experience turned into a painful fiasco. The person to whom you tell the story does not have to be part of the problem. He or she doesn't have to know about the event or the people who were involved in it. He or she need only be trustworthy and a good listener. In my definition, a good listener needs to be non-judgmental and trustworthy. You want to know that they will not use your story by telling it to others or by judging you. You may have somebody in mind who is just perfect for this job, and all you need is to ask him or her to meet you at the appropriate time and place. If you have a friend who fits only part of your definition of a good listener, it may be a good idea to check "the terms of the contract" before you meet. For example, you may know a person who can keep a secret but tends to take sides or pass judgment. You can ask that friend directly to withhold comment for another time, if he or she really wants to help you. Remember that most friends will feel very honored by your choice of them. You may feel that you are burdening them with your troubles or that they may have enough troubles of their own. The truth is that for most people the mere activity of listening to you and feeling helpful will not only give them a boost but may also help them indirectly—by hearing your experience and struggle. As a psychologist, I have often experienced the benefit of being a privileged listener. It is truly an honor.

Despite All Odds: Uncovering Your Survival Skills

As discussed earlier, your mind is well equipped to alert you to pain, bad news, and nerve-racking and demoralizing experiences. Now, we will turn to another exercise in which you try to determine how you have survived your problems so far without making matters worse. Do it only if you like the challenge and are willing to stop feeling sorry for yourself. In this exercise you are asked to wonder why you are not in much worse condition. You may say: It is bad enough as it is and I don't need it any worse. You are right. Yet, it could and would be much worse without your drive for psychohealth and the partial solutions you have already implemented along the way. In this regard, every failure is preceded and followed by an aspiration. To uncover your psychohealth mechanisms, I suggest you think through and write down your answers to the following questions (a series of questions I have borrowed from my colleagues Michael White from Australia and Baruch Sholem from Jerusalem):

- What makes you thrive in the face of a certain difficult challenge, while being knocked out and defeated by other stresses? After so many unsuccessful attempts to overcome the problem, what has allowed you to continue to struggle?
- Face the worst. What is the worst that may happen to you as a result of your problem? Say you feel depressed and feel that your life is going nowhere. The worst thing that could happen may be committing suicide. Now, ask yourself what has happened so far that has stopped you from killing yourself? It may be your unwillingness to hurt your loved ones. It may be the realization that problems are reversible—they come and go—whereas death is an irreversible state.
- You are a survivor. What is the most difficult challenge you have faced to date? What characteristics have allowed you to continue the struggle? How did you develop them?
- Life is undoubtedly a very difficult venture. What makes you hang in there? Why don't you give up? What is it in your will to live that keeps you going? What were you aspiring to during all those years of struggle? What are the contributions you want to make during your short visit on this earth?
- After so much struggling, what have the painful times taught you about self-respect? What would be the next step in developing that respect?

Utilizing the Hidden Observer

People often come to therapy to tell the stories which have become their lives, their reality, their primary identity. Once you have finished telling your story, and a friend has listened to you and understood you, you may be interested in taking it one step further: to edit your story. In a way, the hidden therapist's ultimate goal is to help you reauthor your life by writing an alternative story.

You can start with the present story you just wrote or told in the opening-up exercise, or continue with the series of questions and answers from the exercise on page 111. Eventually what you are trying to do is sort your story out in order to identify a central theme, dilemma or metaphor. Because you are the main character of your story as well as the one who tells it, you may lack the necessary perspective or the fresh eye of a newcomer. You are part of your story and the story has become you. If you feel stuck and overwhelmed, you are probably overlooking certain elements that may reveal a possible alternative role in the story. You may want to create a different emphasis. Review events and relationships in order to include, exclude, or conclude differently.

As people get more and more involved in their personal problems and the failed attempts to solve them, they tend to become part of the problem and cannot separate their perceptions from the actual events. They become their stories. In the following exercise you will review the story about your problem from the point of view of the observer. You will try to externalize the problem so that you can gain some distance and a different perspective on the problem. As you edit or rewrite your story think about the following questions:

- When did you decide that this is your problem? Why?
- What gave the other protagonist(s) of the story so much power over your life?
- What made the problem significant for you?
- Who else is worried about the problem?
- What (or who) helps you prevail?

- How does the problem affect you?
- Can you recall the times when the problem did not exist? When?
- What was unique or different during the period when the problem did not exist?

Now, think for a moment about the whole process from the time the problem started till now. Look at the situation as if you are watching a movie or reading a novel—as if you are looking at your life from the outside.

- If you were to give the story a title, what would it be? What would be the subtitle?
- Write a new ending to the story. Make it a reliable and believable ending. Make it an ending that leaves the viewer with a renewed sense of hope.
- What will be the alternative story? What kind of script will you write for yourself years from now when the problem is over?
- Would you add any new characters, settings, or locations?

Such questions aim to help you gain perspective and an ability to look at your story from the outside in order to realize you can edit it by inclusions, exclusions, and new conclusions, altering your viewpoint. It will still be your story and a true story: one that you reauthored.

Have a Good Laugh at Yourself

Where everything else fails, humor can help. When people can laugh at themselves, everything seems lighter. Good jokes are often about serious and sometimes even sad topics. When you act as the stand-up comedian about your own problem, you can take the problem more lightly and find a new way to view it. A good joke takes a problem and gives it a new perspective by pushing it to an extreme that makes it look absurd or ridiculous. What is often perceived as tragedy is extremely close to comedy—just as a very thin line separates an act of genius from an act of lunacy. In the next exercise you are asked to use "reverse psychology"— instead of trying to solve your problem you will attempt to blow it up into funny or grotesque proportions. For example, if your problem is that you compulsively bite your nails, take a full hour to sit in front of a big mirror and bite all ten of your fingernails one by one, watching yourself and doing it elaborately and seriously. If you are anxious or phobic about meetings or dating and you tend to perspire excessively before such events, encourage yourself to perspire excessively. "Last time I sweat only on my forehead and under my arms. This time I'll sweat all over my body." Such directives may evoke good laughter but also will make an undesired and involuntary act into a voluntary one.

If you find it hard to use reverse psychology on your problem and have a good laugh at yourself, you may want to pick a book, movie, television show, or video that will make you laugh whole-heartedly. Good laughter is one of the best medicines.

Doing Nothing for a Change

In the next exercise I suggest that you decide to do nothing what-soever to solve the problem for the next week. Simply leave it to coincidence or luck to do the job for you. If it bothers you to do nothing, you can remind yourself that you will go back to dealing with it next week. If this is what you have been doing already, please skip this exercise. It works only when it is different from what you have been doing so far. Doing nothing as a result of helplessness, apathy, or destructive denial can hardly be helpful.

You may have noticed that under pressure, you tend to use your basic instincts for fight or flight. When faced with problems many people tend to either do something about it or forget it—to confront the problem or remove themselves from the scene. You can find what works for you only through trial and error. As in any other true learning situation, the errors are a necessary step for new learning. The guiding principle here is very simple. If what you have done so far works for you, don't fix it. If what you have done in trying to solve a problem doesn't work, just quit doing it. Stopping excessive efforts may even allow you to see what your habitual efforts at a solution are and how a negative, vicious cycle can be broken.

Most problems carry with them attempted solutions. The problem grows as those solutions fail. Ask yourself: What have I done so far to solve the problem? Review your attempts to solve it. If you have repeated an ineffective problem-solving attempt over and over again, you have used the "try harder" or "keep fighting" strategy. Common "fight" reactions are: You try to take care of the problem now. You see yourself as responsible for it. You think a lot about it and take it to heart; you see it as very important. You try and retry everything you can come up with. You worry about it constantly.

Now, you may want to try the "doing nothing" strategy. For people educated in the tradition that if something does not work they should simply try harder, the idea of doing nothing may be a hard one to swallow. The following exercises are optional for those who feel they must do something and will provide them with healthy detours from the problem. If asking you to do nothing is too much and you feel you must keep yourself busy, try the following exercises. These are exercises that allow you to shift your focus away from the problem, not attend to it. Practice them whenever you feel stuck, caught in a vicious cycle, or experience the pain of the problem. It is most appropriate for those who tend to get anxious by worrying too much, thinking too hard, and doing a zillion things to keep themselves going.

- TAKE A WALK: When you get stuck in endless fights with your spouse, child, boss, or if you are simply driving yourself insane with fruitless or compulsive efforts to solve your problem, you may need a short walk. Don't spend time getting into the "right" sports clothes or driving to the nicest hiking trail in your state. Just take a ten- to twenty-minute walk around the block as a way of giving yourself a break. Concentrate on the movement of your body—the movement of your legs and arms or your breathing. Feel your feet on the ground, notice your immediate surroundings, and soften your vision to relax your gaze and your forehead.

- PRACTICE YOUR FAVORITE PHYSICAL EXERCISE: Pick the time of day when you are most likely to feel stress or experience the problem most severely and spend half an hour prior to this time doing your favorite physical activity. Do it a bit more rigorously than usual. You could walk, swim, jog, do aerobics, or play a ball game with your friends. This approach is a proactive, preventive way of facing the problem in an indirect fashion. For example, my interpersonal problems used to flare up as I came home from work, especially on Friday nights after an intensive week of work. At work, much of my time is spent listening to other people. Coming home, I did not want to do more of the same. My wife, who was spending all day with little children, looked forward to talking with an adult or she may have needed me to take over or solve problems. Our interactions quickly began to deteriorate. As I approached home through the traffic rush hour, the tension would build up. Only when I decided to leave work half an hour earlier, having worked through my lunch break, did I find I could create a buffer and an appropriate transition between work and home with a non-listening, non-interpersonal activity. Now I swim fifty laps after work. This brings me home in a bit more balanced or relaxed state of mind. You may prefer some other activity: physical, spiritual, social, or otherwise. The point is, whatever you do should be different in content and style from what you have been doing at work. It should not be a direct attempt to discuss or solve the problem.

- NURTURING: If you are not the physical type, you can replace the previous exercise with another nurturing activity that is unrelated to your problem. The idea here is that most problems can improve by shifting or reducing the stress level. Stress in most cases is a message that change or a new situation is needed. In my experience, stress is often a call for me to take better care of myself. A sense of self-care can be achieved immediately by giving your body a simple sense of pleasure. For me, this is through contact with water. When I take a long shower, sit beside a brook, or take a walk on the beach, I immediately experience a different flow in my body. You might feel it in massage, masturbation, dressing up, or listening to music. All of these activities, especially if you do them regularly, will greatly reduce anxiety and support the natural process of change.

- SPACING-OUT, MEDITATION, OR SELF-HYPNOSIS: Meditative and trancelike states of mind occur naturally in everyday life.

Often when you daydream in a boring class, routine job, or while driving on a straight highway, you actually find yourself in a trance state. Deeper trances may take place during a movie, love-making, or listening to music. As shown in Professor Herbert Benson's studies at Harvard University Medical School, such mental states are helpful in a very wide range of conditions from simple stress to severe heart attacks and cancer.

The above exercises are not limited to interpersonal or stress-related problems. They can be useful in other states of mind. For example, in vague emotional states when you can't concentrate or focus on one thing, meditation can help you to center yourself. Physical excercise can help lift a depressive state of mind.

Developing Abilities by Paying Attention

The way people pay attention defines their use of psychic energy and determines the kind of self they are cultivating—the kind of person they are learning to be. When people give their full attention to something—work, play, a relationship—when they are really paying attention, they are calling on all of their resources of intelligence, feeling, and moral sensitivity. At these times, people are not thinking about themselves in isolation because they are completely absorbed in what they are doing. For example, when I take my kids to the playground, all I need to do in order to ensure the optimal quality of my parenting is to pay attention, stay alert, and concentrate on them. Distractions get worse when I begin to interpret, make judgments on, and give meanings to my lack of concentration. Contrary to psychodynamic beliefs, it is less important why and how a person loses concentration. All that is needed is to focus efforts on the relevant area. In my case, I need to go back to concentrating on my kids.

When I succeed, I know I'm "in the game." When I fail, I know I'm still learning. When I am not paying attention, I stop enjoying my kids, I don't enjoy my parenting, and worse yet, I don't enjoy anything. The right act is to focus on the relevant area again and again, as long as needed, until the ability develops to the level that allows you to enjoy yourself.

Everyone has a rich repertoire of abilities that can be used to ignore and pass through disturbances, distractions, and self-doubt. Once you feel competent in what you do, you spend less and less energy fighting your lapses in concentration. As you improve, you enjoy and express yourself more fully. The more you enjoy the activity, the less you lose concentration. You feel more present and invested in your abilities, your projects, and your relationships.

If you are someone who is introspective, psychologically minded, and sensitive, you may need to shift your attention. Instead of concentrating on how you feel about yourself, you need to develop your ability to get out of your inner walls. For example, when you concentrate on a lecture, a book, your job, the person in front of you, to the extent that you forget about yourself, this is when you begin to enjoy yourself. You enjoy yourself because you add something new to your repertoire right now. When you are stuck with yourself and concentrating wholly on how you feel, check to see if you are walking in a closed and vicious cycle.

Focusing on what will happen to you ten years from now is not relevant. It does not matter if you intend to start a diet tomorrow or be a successful businessperson ten years from now. If you don't translate your vague plan into some action now, you may lose the very thing you wish to do in the future. You want to take whatever small steps are possible now.

Use this chapter for encouragement to:

• Improve your ability to solve your problem now.

• Define as a non-problem—for a week at least—whatever you are unable to solve by "trying harder."

• Pay attention to your present task and surroundings. Do not repress or deny your present life; concentrate on your very immediate future.

The next few days may be part of your present. Treat them as if they were all you have. Do not waste too much time crying over your mistakes and failures, even those that seem severe. Move ahead the way you do when you drive. How far do you need to see ahead in order to drive well? What happened on this road in the past is irrelevant. What is going to happen a few miles or hours down the road will not improve your driving right now. At most, you need to notice the car right behind you, and what is right in front of you, which is the view to your most immediate future.

The continued construction and reconstruction of self and the uncovering of the pathways to your potential is a very exciting adventure. This is more or less all anyone is capable of doing. It may not seem like much, but it is a lot. You can continue this venture on your own, as well as with trusted friends or partners. During the times when you feel as if you are failing, I invite you to consider single-session therapy as your next step.

5

Making the Most of the First—or Only—Session

Ruth is in her late fifties and is significantly overweight. She had what she considered an uncontrolled desire for chocolate, cookies, and cakes. She had tried many diets, with limited and short-lived success. She came to my office with her husband, a distinguished professor. I let him wait and invited her into my office. She told me her story of thirty years of failed attempts to lose weight. I said: "You have been struggling with this problem for a long time. What makes you come to see me now?"

"I read about your work with single-session therapies in a magazine article. I felt I wanted to take care of my weight now without the grueling charts, tasteless diets, and a repeated sense of failure. It makes me feel stupid and helpless."

"Are you expecting some hocus-pocus to happen in a single session?"

She laughed and said, "Who doesn't? But I also know that even after the best of all single sessions, tomorrow will come and I'll see cakes and chocolate somewhere and will have to respond differently than I usually do."

"How would you know if magic really happened and you could feel good about your weight after today?" I asked.

"I would be able to see sweets through a shield of indifference. And if that doesn't work I'd still be able to go to the beach and not give a damn about what other people think about my body when I'm wearing a bathing suit." She was reframing the either/or dilemma in terms of an and/both solution.

The rest of the session I focused on all the attempts she had made throughout her life to go on a diet. What was most encouraging was her ability to feel sexy and loved by her husband and his reassurance that he loves her as she is. As was accurately noted by Roberta Russell in her book with R. D. Laing, *R. D. Laing & Me: Lessons in Love:* "It is not the lack of knowing what to do that prevents the wistful but unsuccessful dieter from sticking to an appropriate eating and exercise routine. . . . The most readily available source for mastery of our own good advice must be an empathic, purposeful relationship with another human being." (In SST it is critical to identify a co-therapist—often a beloved partner—who helps you see your way clear to solutions without developing undue dependency.) I decided to use hypnosis to provide a ritual of "hocus-pocus" to create a bridge between the available resource of her loving relationship with her husband and her image of creating a shield between her and sweets. All my inductions and metaphors were taken from her story as she told it and were full of suggestions about both her ability to love and be loved as she is and her readiness to find her right weight and create a shield between herself and the sweets. I suggested that she had come to see me now because she was ready to lose weight and keep it off for as long as she wanted.

When I pulled her out of the trance I asked her husband to join us. It was apparent that he was an available resource and a potential co-therapist. I stressed again that Ruth's timing in coming to see me was perfect because she was now ready to do something new and effective to deal with her weight problem. I told them how impressed I was by the sense of love and commitment they had for one another. I suggested that until she was sure that cakes and chocolates had no influence on her diet, he should support her by not having any cakes and chocolates at home or by "doing something else sweet together" when they go out. Meanwhile, she was to take whatever fit her from our session and let go of the rest. Until she was ready to face sweets differently, I suggested she go to the beach with her grandchildren, wearing her bathing suit, and concentrate on playing with her grandchildren, enjoying their presence. Before ending the session, I asked Ruth how long she would need in order to lose enough weight to convince herself that she was doing well. She replied that she would need six weeks. We set a follow-up phone call for two months later, "just in case you need two extra weeks to reach your goal."

In the follow-up phone conversation, Ruth said: "I am very pleased. I lost twenty pounds. Better yet, chocolates and sweets have no effect on me, as if there is a screen between me and the table full of goodies. It is amazing because I don't even have to struggle with the wish to eat them. Yesterday I went to a big party with all the goodies in the world. I ate none and it was effortless. Throughout the two months I ate well and kept to a balanced diet without any special program."

"It sounds like magic. It's hard to believe. What has changed since our session?" I asked.

"It *was* like magic," Ruth replied. "One hour after the session and thereafter I could stand the temptation. We went to restaurants and stores filled with sweets and cakes. I hosted people and served them everything. It is remarkable. I don't even have to struggle. I enjoy it."

"Did anybody else notice a difference?"

"My husband and sons are still surprised by my radical and sudden change. They keep saying how impressed they are with me."

"What made it all possible?"

"I think it was the timing. If I had come to see you one week earlier or one week later it might not have worked as well. It was perfect timing. I can't explain it any other way. It was just the perfect time. I was ready and you were the right therapist at the right time."

The importance of Ruth's story is not SST as the latest diet trick; rather, it is to show that even a very severe or serious problem that has never been treated by psychotherapy can be solved in a very brief, profoundly useful session as long as the client is ready to do something different, now. How can you realize when the time is right for you? You can examine your readiness, which is your internal, idiosyncratic state of immediate preparedness and willingness to take the necessary steps toward a satisfactory resolution.

Pick a specific problem you are having and ask yourself on a scale from 0 to 100 percent:
- How important is it for you to solve the problem now?
- How motivated are you?
- How active and committed are you in regard to solving the specific problem?
- How urgent or painful is the problem to you?

Another way to evaluate your readiness is to notice any spontaneous changes and activities once you have identified the problem or sought help. Improvements facilitated by hope, faith, or expectation suggest inner readiness for a corrective experience.

Making the Most of the First (and Often Only) Session

The best form of therapy, for most people in most cases, is the least restrictive and least intrusive. Single-session therapy, the briefest possible therapy, has the potential to be the least restrictive and least intrusive. All lengths and forms of therapy should have one main goal: to help you to help yourself. In other words, therapy should help you to become independent of your therapist as soon as possible and it should restore your sense that you can manage on your own. At the same time you need to be aware that you can reconnect to your therapist whenever necessary.

The therapeutic alliance works best when you trust the therapist to be there for you for as long as necessary, while you work to make her or him unnecessary as soon as possible. Long-term therapists believe that you need first to depend on them or develop a strong attachment (they call this dependence "transference feelings"), so that you will later separate and become independent in healthier ways than you experienced before. In contrast, the brief therapist asks, "What is the most efficient and practical way I can help this client today, so he or she can go back to the business of life?" For the long-term therapist, your "transference feelings" are the main tool for working with you and gaining "insight" to your "deeper" problems in your relationship to a parental figure. The brief therapist is an immediate, present facilitator of your innate abilities.

What happens in SST? How can talking to somebody just one time help?

SST does not use magic or tricks. It is not a one-size-fits-all solution. It is helpful because it is simple, practical, and immediately useful. It is based on the belief that most people only need to be shown the switch, and they will turn the light on by themselves. When provided with the turning point, most people will travel the rest of the road on their own.

Some therapists may have trouble realizing when enough is enough, when to let go. It is left to the clients to decide just that and to leave therapy and go on with their lives without undue dependencies and expenses. SST recognizes that no one is perfect or totally immune from bad luck and undue pain. Everyone knows that these elements are part of life. Most people know that no amount of money or therapy will make them free of pain or make them happy once and for all. It is good enough to know and trust that there is a simple and inexpensive way to cope with personal problems. It is also important that people keep in the back of their minds the option to utilize the therapist again if and when necessary.

The First-Time Chemistry

In your first (and perhaps only) therapeutic encounter, much can be accomplished. The fresh start between people who have never met before and have the same goal in mind creates a powerful therapeutic potential, which goes beyond any theories, techniques, or logical explanations. There is something about the first time, which happens only once and is never repeated. Something that may seem magical can occur in the first meeting of two minds, two personalities. As Carl Jung put it in his book *Memories, Dreams, Reflections:* "The meeting of two personalities is like the contact of two chemical substances: If there is any reaction both are transformed."

Seeing a therapist is rarely like seeing other professionals. You are not there because your car died this morning or because it's tax season again. The first psychotherapy session is rarely a response to a new problem that started yesterday. Undoubtedly, you have coped with the problem for quite some time and have tried various ways to solve it. Psychotherapy is a last resort. (For example, the average time lapse between the first symptoms of panic attacks and seeking psychological help is twelve years, as discussed by Nikki Meredith in her article "Testing the Talking Cure.") Most important, the problem has to do with you. Despite all your shortcomings and blind spots, nobody knows about you and your problem as much as you do. What you bring to the first session is unique, special, and essential. The long road you traveled to the first session has also been governed by the immense wisdom and power of your mental immune system.

The Built-in Drive to Health

In our study (discussed in the introduction to this book), my colleagues and I found that prior to the first session the mental immune system and problem-solving capacities often enter into vigorous action. Many of my single-session clients arrive at the first session with spontaneous and inner knowledge about what they need to do. Clients tell how once they recognized the problem and acknowledged the need to consult a professional they started to find answers and experience improvements even prior to the first session. All the therapist needs to do is use his or her status and experience to validate, encourage, and facilitate the client's inner knowledge and bring it from potential to actuality, from becoming to being, from thought to action. As a client, you need to remember that you traveled a long road to the first session and will continue on whatever road you choose long after the last session.

Traditionally, all that a therapist wants to accomplish in the first session is "intake": to gather information about you. For your sake, be in charge of your part in the session and save your judgments of the therapist's behavior for later. The point is how well *you* come out of the session; your therapist is not up for evaluation. You want to make the most out of your first session now. In this chapter I will show you how to provide the therapist with the most useful and practical information for making SST the most effective it can be, and I will provide guidelines for steering a session toward solutions.

Three elements will determine the success of your first session:
- How open and true to yourself you are in the first session.
- How clear and well-focused you can become in the course of the first session in describing your agenda and sticking to it so that therapy does not quickly become a vague and diffuse conversation about whatever comes to mind; creating a focus is often an effective antidote to overwhelming feelings.
- Your ability to liberate (usually prior to the first session or right after it) your hidden therapist, that is, your built-in drive to achieve mental and physical health. (This is discussed in depth in chapter 4.)

The job of the therapist is to be wise, competent, and trustworthy. The therapist does this by:
- Listening, understanding, and relating to you.

- Identifying and amplifying useful changes and existing strengths.
- Removing, effectively and efficiently, the obstructions that presently block you from growing in your chosen direction.

To illustrate single-session therapy in action, let's take the story of Jay, who came to see me with the opening statement of, "I'm a complete failure." What can you do in one session with such a devastating feeling? Not much, it would seem. But just a little bit of change can go a long way. A small success can breed larger ones. Furthermore, the art of SST is to differentiate between the problems that can be solved and those that can't. It is helpful to pay attention only to what you are able and ready to change or do now.

Jay, 30, had never married and worked as an independent distributor of meat products. "I'm nobody and I've accomplished nothing in life. Every customer I have and every woman I wish to date can see right through my insecurities." He described a long history of failures in his social and personal life.

"When you become somebody who has accomplished something in life, how would that be different than your present life?" I asked.

"I'd be married with kids," he quickly replied.

When I inquired further, I found out that Jay had been raised by a violent father and a psychotic mother hardly able to take care of Jay, since she was in and out of touch with reality. He never saw any expression of love at home. He never felt appreciated for anything. He dropped out of high school, tried unsuccessfully to make friends, and was continuously rejected by women he tried to date. He felt at a total loss for interpersonal and social skills, demoralized nearly to the core. I inquired about his past, looking for a thread of self-respect or hope.

"What do you feel you have accomplished, that your parents did not?"

He described his success in always holding a job and finally being able to afford to buy a small apartment for himself, something his father was never able to do. He described his struggle not to lose touch with reality and not to get violent. He felt he had just barely succeeded. Many times he felt tempted to release the tremendous tension and frustration he held inside with the same violence he had suffered from in his childhood. To learn other models of behavior and coping, he had gone to growth seminars but had not been able to implement those experiences into his daily life. For a traditional therapist the model and approach would be to concentrate on all that had gone wrong in his childhood and explain to him how it affected his present life. Instead, I chose to search for a viable current solution to the deep hopelessness he felt and his lack of self-confidence.

Matching a Solution to a Problem

I wanted Jay to experience even some small sense of success and accomplishment. He was hardworking and responsible in his job and I felt that his work provided a context through which he might feel even more competent. I wanted him to confront his problem with social skills in a setting where he could experience some success.

I learned from the creative therapist, Bradford Keeney (in his book *Improvisational Therapy*) that instead of trying to help people to find a whole new solution to their problem, therapy can help them by matching a solution that has proved successful in one realm with a problem in another realm. Paraphrasing Keeney, I said to Jay: "You were clear in defining the problem. You have also indicated a history of experiencing one failure after another in your efforts to find a solution. This history of experienced failures concerns me. With every failure, you set up a situation in which you have less faith and confidence in your ability to create an effective solution. With this loss of confidence, whether you're aware of it or not, the creative part of your mind becomes more reluctant to try again. Clearly, the solution to your problem *can* come from you. What we must do *now* is get your creative mind to have more confidence in its ability to come up with the appropriate solution.

"There is a way! Each attempted solution you may have previously tried is, in fact, evidence of your strengths, which can be gathered and used for an appropriate, creative solution for some other problem. You need to figure out what problems would be solved by previous solutions you've tried in various arenas. When you experience these solutions as successful in solving other problems, your creative mind will become confident again. That's more than half the battle. Every solution must find the problem that fits it; then you can move on to another solution to solve a different problem."

Jay and I selected, after some discussion in this one session and in follow-up phone calls, two solutions he had tried before to solve his problem in dating women—putting an ad in the personal section of a local paper and trying to sweet-talk complete strangers into dating him—and applied them to another problem he had in expanding his business to new stores and clientele. He found himself less combative and uptight when he approached these clients as though they were potential friends. In a follow-up phone call he told me that he had increased his volume of business by more than 50 percent and that a woman he liked had approached him and they had been steadily dating for four months. "She is great. She understands and knows how to handle me well," he said. Was it SST or luck that the woman approached Jay? I hope it was a combination of both that got Jay unstuck. Don't be mistaken: Jay's life was not "happy ever after" following SST. He had many challenges to face and many more problems to solve. At one point, sixteen months after our session, he returned to see me with his new wife for brief marriage counseling.

I am often asked in workshops and interviews: What do you actually do in SST? How is it different from regular therapy? No two single-session therapy sessions are exactly the same. Effective SST needs to be tailored to the special situation. The suggested solution needs to fit the client's abilities, attitudes, and preferences.

I present here some of the questions most commonly asked during SST. They provide an illustration to help demystify the process of SST. These are the questions I ask and they reflect the way I conduct single-session therapy. They represent only some of the many possibilities.

The questions in the section below help the SST therapist to learn your view and your experience of the problem and to search for the most desirable solution. As a therapist, I assume that both the knowledge and the healer are within you, not in me; all I try to do is ask questions that bring this knowledge and healing capacity into the open where they will be more accessible.

These are the attitudes and emphases you should look for if you want a therapist oriented toward brief therapy. These are also the sorts of questions you can ask yourself and directions toward which you can encourage yourself.

The First Step: When You Call for Help

When you make the first step by picking up the phone and calling to request help, the therapist should be available as soon as possible. There are more than 200,000 professional therapists in the United States alone, and in most large communities there is a surplus of therapists utilizing a wide range of methods. This variety and the competition for clients allow you to demand high-quality care. You should look for a therapist who is responsive, attentive, and accessible from the outset. You may have pondered for quite some time before finding the courage to call a therapist and you may feel embarrassed by your problem or just by asking for help. The pre-session phone conversation is an integral and critical part of successful SST.

When you call for an initial appointment, therapy is already under way. You have already identified some aspect of the problem as needing change and started the steps (choosing a therapist, making a phone call) that you hope will promote change. Your therapist can channel this movement by setting the stage for constructive SST. First he or she wants to bring the right players into the session. This includes everybody who wants to and can be part of the solution. At times, the individual who calls for help can solve the problem himself or herself. On other occasions, other key players can make a difference. It could be a lover, a friend, a spouse, or an employer. Therapy may include an individual, a couple, or a group of people. The key question is not who has the problem, but who has the solution, who are the agents of change? Once the therapist identifies the solution team, he or she wants them to join forces in a way that will enable every participant to contribute to a viable solution, or at least come out of the session better off than they were before the session. Some callers will tell the therapist about the problem right away. If they do, the SST therapist will listen attentively and interrupt little. If they wait for guiding questions, the SST therapist may ask the following questions. (These are also questions you can ponder yourself.)

"What made you decide to call me now?" or: *"What made you decide that now is the right time for therapy?"*

The *why now?* questions, as discussed in the last chapter, help you identify a specific motivation, trigger, or leverage for change. You are most likely to change when you can no longer go on using the old ways. Once you recognize a problem and identify the specific motivation or need for change, you are well on your way toward finding a workable solution.

"Who else is worried, caring, or trying to help out with the problem?"

This question suggests that you may not be the only one who sees a problem and wishes to solve it. You can search for co-helpers and co-therapists in your daily environment. If you bring co-therapists or active clients into the first therapy session, you may have more alternatives and more potential for change. Potential customers are those who wish to change the situation or are willing to be a part of the solution. Customers will do more than complain or simply pay a visit to a therapist. They come to do more than to be heard or hear what the therapist has to say. They are active customers who get the best service by being part of the solution. Therapy often fails if the participants try to change somebody else or only wish to complain about life.

"How and how soon would you like to be helped?" or: *"How and how soon do you expect the problem to be solved?"*

"How" and "how soon" suggest actions and a time frame for therapy. These questions also suggest that you are involved in a supportive relationship, aimed at solving a problem in an efficient and time-limited fashion. When I started to conduct psychotherapy,

I assumed that all patients needed at least several years of once-a-week, open-ended therapy. Once I stopped taking my clients for granted and asked the above questions in the initial contact, I realized that many people wish for ad hoc help that certainly can occur, in most cases, in one to five sessions.

Others may wish for more, but time and money constraints often limit therapy to a few sessions. The interesting fact is that therapy takes exactly the length of time you allocate for it. When you and the therapist expect change to happen now—it often does!

The SST therapist asks you to set your goal and to make a schedule for taking care of it. Jenny suffered from panic and anxiety attacks. When I asked her how soon she would like to be helped, she replied immediately, "yesterday!" and explained that her coming to see me was long overdue. Now when clients reply by saying "yesterday" or "now," or that they expect results within a few sessions, I challenge them to take action and use the first session in order to take the necessary turn. If the client responds by saying "I have no idea" or "for as long as I need you", that indicates open-ended or time-unlimited therapy.

Fostering Readiness

Before ending the pre-session phone conversation the SST therapist may add a final statement, which is meant to be hope-inspiring and self-fulfilling. In my years of work as a therapist I have learned that therapy is to a large extent a self-fulfilling process in which you can take almost any problem and make it a subject for endless and open-ended therapy. By the same token, therapists can set expectations that enable clients to take care of the problem right now.

Whatever time and context you provide for solving a problem

will be the time needed. Here is an example of what the SST therapist may say at the end of the initial call:

"I'm willing to work with you toward a satisfying solution of your problem. I believe you called me today because now is the time to take the necessary steps to solve the problem. You may be able to resolve your problem before, during, or right after the first visit. I trust you are willing to do whatever is necessary now to bring about change, and that you are willing to work hard for it. I'll do everything I can and will work with you whenever it is necessary. I see my job as helping you to help yourself. I see your job as making me obsolete as soon as possible. In most cases I see people from one to three sessions. I expect to make your therapy as brief as possible."

Of course, you can't put words into your therapist's mouth. But you can convey that this is how you want your therapy to be focused, and see if your therapist is open to that approach. If the idea of SST surprises your therapist, you could suggest proceeding one session at a time. A mutually agreed-upon SST is the best scenario.

How Would You Like to Be Helped?

You want to clarify how you want the therapist to help you. Three of the most common things a therapist can do for you are: suggest a solution to a problem; listen empathetically and understand the depth of your experience; give professional perspective or guidance.

Each of these things requires different skills and behavior from the therapist. To listen and understand requires the therapist to be more attentive and perceptive by listening and letting you do most of the talking. A therapist who is asked to solve a problem or to give guidance needs to be direct and active. She or he asks more questions, makes more suggestions, and steers the session to bring you to a point where her or his advice will be best suited and most useful to your present situation and available resources.

You may think you want open-ended therapy but find after a few sessions that you don't need it anymore. Sharon complained of loneliness and isolation and sought open-ended therapy with me. She said, "I need to know that you are there for me and I can always call you." The only time she didn't feel lonely was during the church choir rehearsals she attended once a week. I gave her a task: to notice times and places where she was alone, but not lonely (e.g., listening to music in her apartment), and times when she was not alone and not lonely (e.g., during the choir rehearsal). After the third session she already had two people she felt were "good listeners and there for me." Sharon was able to use therapy to identify an exception and turn it into a rule. Therapy was terminated at her request after five sessions.

The length of therapy is clearly going to be determined by many factors, some (but not all) of which are in your control. These include your motivation and sense of urgency, but also the time and money you have available to put into this venture. Let the therapist tell you if she or he has the tools and skills to help you within the parameters you describe. You may need a few minutes to negotiate the contract or reframe the goals so that they are more likely to be attainable within your timetable. You can't ask the therapist to make you happy or change your personality in one session. No wise therapist will promise you that.

When you have reached an understanding, restate and affirm your goal. In therapy, as in life, there are no guarantees, but it's helpful to have a clear understanding of what you want and what the therapist can offer. "I want to live in harmony and be happy," said Wendy when I asked her what she would like to accomplish in therapy.

"I have been in therapy for years," I replied, "and I'm still searching for harmony and happiness. Will you be kind enough to call me as soon as you have found harmony and happiness? I would like it too."

The Beginner's Mind

When people walk into my office for the first time, I try to be as fresh and open-minded as I can. I want to keep a beginner's mind and be able to feel all the anxieties, hopes, and fears brought to the first session. I remind myself that no SST looks like the last one and no solution is universal. In some sessions I act mostly as a listener, letting the client get everything off his or her chest, telling his or her story from beginning to end, with almost no interruptions. I ask only minor questions to make sure I understood the main messages correctly. In other sessions I am very active, guiding clients with my questions, persuading and using my best rhetoric and inductions to convince my clients to change their minds. I may shift gears as I observe the reactions of my patients. I lead the session by responding to the verbal and non-verbal cues and reactions of my clients.

The scheme of questions and statements presented here is based on some themes that tend to reemerge often in my SSTs. This material is intended to help people regain a sense of mastery in their lives and rewrite their stories to introduce more hope, higher morale, and more positive feelings. I believe that with the right perspective you'll realize that there are many ways to solve your problem. With the knowledge and feeling that you have options, you will make the right selection as soon as you're ready. Until now I've described common issues which are discussed mainly in the initial phone call prior to the SST. The following questions are raised during the actual session. Again, these are the kinds of issues you can ponder yourself and/or raise with the therapist.

Noticing and Encouraging Change

"You initially called me two weeks ago. What changes have you noticed in the past two weeks?"

The process of change is already under way and the only question is whether you were able to notice it. This is like saying, "We all have dreams at night. Some of us recall them and some don't." In this way the SST therapist reestablishes the expectation, the belief that change takes place all the time and important changes happen outside of the session. That expectation is likely to lead to awareness of those changes. (You can, of course, work on making this shift in attitude yourself.) Furthermore, with such a question the therapist can follow up on the pre-session changes. If the mood or the problem has changed since the initial contact, the therapist can start the session where the client is right now, instead of where he or she was during the initial phone call. Remember that some therapists will not take the time to talk to you prior to the first session. You can insist on a pre-session conversation or you can rehearse by having an internal conversation in which you try to figure out your expectations. In any case, tell your therapist about the pre-session changes.

"What would you would like to accomplish today?"

With this question the SST therapist tries to let you know that therapy is a business transaction dealing with your present possibilities. It is not small talk. It is a process of achieving a goal and not just a chance to express your troubles and complaints to a sympathetic ear. Getting things "off your chest" may be a necessary first step in therapy and it is a useful one as long as you are willing to move on with your life and not get caught in a cycle of self-pity. There is nothing wrong with paying a therapist to get a sympathetic ear; just don't lose sight of the fact that it all has the purpose of improving your life and solving your problem.

Your first job is to explain to the therapist what it is you would like to accomplish now and that you are ready to achieve that. You want to bring your agenda forward right from the start. If you have done this during the initial phone conversation, start the session by telling the therapist about the changes that have taken place since you talked on the phone. As a result of those pre-session changes, your attitude or your main concern itself may have changed. Let the therapist know about these right from the start; otherwise the therapist will only gather the history and description of the problem.

"What will convince you that you have indeed accomplished what you wanted? How will you know when you don't need me anymore?"

This question guides you to look forward, instead of backward. In stating your goal, start with the most urgent or desired goal and state it in the most specific way you can. Illustrate with examples. Try to break it down into what you want to accomplish first ("I would like first to be back at work"), and what may be your goal in the long run ("I would like to have a more interesting and rewarding career").

If you use labels or generic terms like depression, anxiety, or stress to describe your problem, make sure you tell the therapist what those feelings consist of or what their more specific presentations, settings, or definitions mean to you.

I encourage you to create a specific and detailed vision of your goal. The SST therapist may need to ask a few more questions along these lines until your goal is both attainable and specific enough, so that you can measure your progress. The therapist will help you to find the courage to change what you can and to acknowledge what you can't change.

Building Up Readiness and Motivation

If the therapist sees you as a potential SST client—or if you want to set this up yourself— with a reliable hope for changing now, he or she—or you—may specifically present the possibility of SST by saying:

"Many people who come to therapy do so for only one session and find that to be helpful and sufficient. If we need more sessions, we can schedule them at the end of today's session or whenever you may need to in the future. But what we'll do today is try to get to the bottom of your problem and look for helpful solutions. Is that what you had in mind?"

An alternative statement may sound like:

"When you are ready, but not before, I'll be glad to meet with you for one, two, or three sessions. I believe that when both of us are prepared to take care of business now, a lot can be accomplished in a very short time."

The key message here conveys that change can occur immediately and that the client has the most power when seizing the moment to make a difference in his or her life.

When Jenny told me about her ten years of struggle with constant anxieties and very complex problems, I said to her at the end of the first session, "You brought to me a very complex problem, which has a very simple solution." I felt this would be an encouraging, and not a demeaning, statement because it seemed evident that she was ready to get rid of her anxieties now. I also wanted her to reduce the sense of being overwhelmed which is often the case with anxiety. I asked her to write a detailed letter to her mom in which she could tell her some of the painful lessons she had learned in the last ten years, and explain why she is now ready to move on with her life and reduce the anxieties to a level where they will serve as her "parenting guidance" to make mature decisions. She called me six months later to report significant progress and consulted me on a critical decision she had to make regarding her career. We had two very targeted single sessions, six months apart.

It is also important, though, not to rush the process or create false expectations. Trying too hard, too fast is the best way to undermine your success.

Some patients may not like the idea of change because of its implication that something is presently wrong or bad. They may want to think about the first session as "brainstorming" or may want to "learn" or "create" something new. If a client has carried the problem for many years before seeking help through therapy, the SST therapist promotes readiness by saying:

"So, it's finally gotten bad enough for you to do something to get rid of this. Are you ready to change or do whatever is necessary now?"

This and other similar statements and questions in SST are intended to foster readiness for change. The SST therapist assumes that in the first session various conditions are near the threshold of possibility for change and can, with the recognition and skillful facilitation of the therapist, be assisted into actuality. For example, you may already have made a move in the right direction by recognizing that you are "stuck" in a destructive relationship. SST will provide "permission" to act on this realization, thus restoring congruency in the psychological triangle of feeling-thinking-action. Once you act in congruency with what you feel and think about your relationship, you may regain a sense of balance and self-mastery in your life.

"How would you know that things are starting to improve, even just a little bit?"

This question guides you to identify a small yet significant first step in the right direction. The therapist may try to get you to visualize the improvement in specific details so you get as clear a picture as possible of such change. Work together on shifting your focus to specifics and away from broad, overwhelming generalizations. The therapist may use visual imagery, hypnosis, role-playing, or discussion to make the possibilities for change more real. A question like this may help you better define your goal and break it down into smaller, more manageable steps.

I asked my first SST client, a mother of two youngsters, to take a very small step. That step seemed to be unrelated to the problem as she presented it, but it was one I hoped would give her a different perspective on her kids. At the time they were like little monsters, and in her words, "Some days I am ready to kill them, they get so deeply under my skin."

I asked her as a start to take two hours a week off from the kids and the household chores and go to a cosmetologist to care for her skin or any part of her body she felt needed better care. She did this, and it gave her a little bit of a break from her kids. Once she did that, a whole series of changes followed. "When I took the time for myself, the boys' behavior stopped getting under my skin. As a result, I started to feel a bit better as a mother, which in turn freed me to take better care of myself. When I started to feel better about my looks and myself, my marriage and sex life improved. And then my husband became more considerate and involved in parenting. So, as you can see, a small change turned out to be quite a big one."

Too good to be true? Well, I thought so too and continued to work harder and go deeper with my other clients, until 250 follow-up phone calls to SST clients convinced me that big problems don't require big solutions. Don't worry. Your small step does not have to change your entire life right away. The woman above gave me her report of successful change a year after the session. It needed that long for smaller changes to accumulate and evolve into a big change. Allow time to help you build up the solution.

Focusing on Strengths, Solutions and Abilities

If things have already started to improve prior to or during the first session, or if you have been able to identify past successes or partially useful solutions, the therapist may take it one step further and ask, or you can ask yourself:

"What made this success (or solution) possible? How would you be convinced that the noticed changes are here to stay?"

Every psychological problem, even the most severe one, has moments when it recedes. It could be times, places, or people who help you behave as if the problem has dissipated. When you can identify such exceptions to the problem, these can later be noticed, amplified, broadened, and underlined to gain more significance. The SST therapist shifts the conversation from problems to solutions, from disabilities to capabilities, from weaknesses to the strengths you have.

When I saw Sue and David they were very discouraged about how Jamie, their son, was performing in school. I asked them to review with me everything they had tried so far. They talked about many things that did not work and how discouragement had led them to seek therapy. We were also able to discuss one teacher who had worked well with both Jamie and his parents in the past. I found out more details about what worked with this teacher and was able to encourage Jamie and his parents to respond to the present teacher as if he were the former teacher. They did not have to change much, only to remember, renew, and reactivate what worked for them in the past. Jamie could neither select nor change his teachers, but he could change the way he responded to them.

What Is Your Real Purpose in Seeking Therapy?

If all of the above questions and suggestions get you nowhere it may be that you don't have any specific problem you wish to change or that what you wish to change is not changeable. SST can be helpful if you just want somebody to listen to your story and tell you if something is wrong with you. ("Do you think I am crazy or what?") Or you may want help in making a decision in a sensitive area of your life where you experience conflict or ambivalence.

Don't expect the therapist to read your mind and walk you through the session with his or her questions. Most have habits and routines based on their training and the paperwork they need to fill out at the end of the session. The therapist's goal is not necessarily your goal!

The two most common mistakes of new clients are waiting for the therapist to read their minds and trying to help her or him by telling everything *they think* the therapist wants to hear. You may be surprised to learn that descriptions of your history and troubles are not necessary for the solution of most problems.

Be clear about what you want the therapist to provide. Is it advice, listening, reassurance, diagnosis, or solution of a problem? A competent therapist should be versatile and flexible enough to adapt to your needs. If you think she or he missed the point, or is trying to sell you something you don't need, don't be polite. Let her or him know what you think.

The process of identifying and amplifying changes is central to successful SST. Yet some people do not come to therapy to change anything. For example, in response to whatever the therapist asks they keep returning to the recitation of their life stories. Then, the therapist may try to pinpoint their true agenda by asking:

"Did you come here today to tell me your story and have me listen to you and understand you?"

Not all clients are clear about what they expect of therapy. This question probes one possibility. If your goal is to tell your side of the story without being interrupted or judged, doing that should be your first step; you should tell your story (granted, this could fill up an entire session or two) and the therapist should listen and ask questions only to communicate that he or she understands the essence of your story and your role in it. When you have finished your story and you feel the therapist has heard and understood you, he or she may ask:

"What is it that you would like to see happening now? What's next?"

You may want the therapist to sympathize with you. You may want her or him to validate your feelings and tell you, "You are not crazy, you are okay." You may want nothing other than to get this story off your chest. Getting it all out and letting go of it may be greatly beneficial. If that is true, you can communicate to the therapist that you have accomplished what you wanted and are ready to wrap up the session. Therapists tend to continue the session for fifty minutes regardless of whether you have something else to say or not. You may want to stop while you are ahead!

Most clients want the therapist to like and understand them. They may use psychiatric terms hoping those will help the situation. But be careful: What a layperson means by depression is often very different from the clinical definition of depression. You may mean that lately you have been feeling the blues and are down on yourself. What a psychiatrist will be wondering at hearing the word "depression" is: Are you a suicide risk? Are your sleep, appetite, and libido disturbed? Are you feeling totally hopeless and helpless about life and yourself?

The more specific and well-focused your language and your goals, the better the chance that your therapist will provide you with what you need and that her or his responses will be guided by your special situation rather than by the routine way of working with new clients. Speak your own language; don't tell the therapist what you think she or he expects to hear. You want the therapist to meet and understand you; you don't want to be another "case" like the one she or he saw yesterday.

If a client is unable to pinpoint a goal, the SST therapist may ask him or her to project into the future. I may ask (and you could work on imagining):

"How will your life look when you don't need therapy anymore? What will it feel like when you are not stressed out? Can you give me an example? As you know, problems come and go. What would you do if a relapse happened? How would you restore your balance?"

Through these questions the SST therapist tries to direct your attention to the fact that problems come and go. Expecting therapy to cure all your problems once and for all will lead to therapy forever. To avoid the feeling of "back to square one" when you experience a setback, try to see each problem as a challenge from which you can gain a new perspective or learn another lesson. Each time you meet the same problem, you will look at it a bit differently as a result of your previous experiences and previous solutions.

Testing Alternative Solutions

After asking the above questions, the SST therapist may now have enough information about what is working (and what is not working) in the client's life. The SST therapist searches for the exceptions, past successes, strengths, hopes, desires, and the available social support system. Tell your therapist about these. He or she will also have some information about what doesn't work, what was discouraging and made the client feel stuck and unable to solve it on his or her own.

Now, the therapist may want to take a break and think about the following question: From all I have learned in this session, what do I think the patient is ready and willing to do now in order to experience a difference or feel hope and desire to take the necessary steps toward a satisfying solution? I search for the solution within my client's life experience, philosophy, capabilities, and available support system (family, friends). If this break does occur, you can be thinking along the same lines.

"Which of the things that work for you (the therapist restates them) are you willing to do more of now? Which of the things that do not work (list them) can you quit doing, or at least do less of?"

SST therapists never underestimate their clients or take them for granted. Later in the SST, the therapist explores potential solutions in "as if" form. The therapist may role-play a confrontation between a man and his father, or he or she may visualize the solution and see how far the patient can go. SST therapists may create different scenarios, like a movie script, and let the client choose the one that fits best. Therapists may create a simulation of driving the car or being at work, and see how the patient responds to alterations in these situations. It is like trying on a variety of clothes to find out what best fits the taste, figure, and budget of the client.

I tried a variety of simulated solutions with Marilyn during our SST together. None of them seemed possible enough. When this happens and you can't change the reality of your life, you can try to change your mind-set about this same reality.

Marilyn told me a long and complicated story about her family of origin and how it is affecting her present life. She is working as a teacher and does not like it, and she has financial problems. Her parents stress values over money and see working for money as participating in the capitalist rat race. When the simulated solution of a new job and better management of her finances seemed unlikely to Marilyn, I asked her to look for the conditions and situations that would show that her cup is half full, instead of half empty. We acknowledged that this was a challenge, that at times her cup might seem to be only one-tenth full, that she would have to use her imagination and shift her focus to fill the gap and see the cup as half full. At follow-up, a month later, Marilyn reported she had had the best month of her life. "It is amazing how simple yet powerful my mind-set can be," she reported. "I decided to look at only the half-full portion of things and everything changed right in front of my eyes. For example, visiting my parents was always a stressful and upsetting event for me. This time I only noticed the beautiful nature surrounding my parents' town, how much my daughter enjoys her grandparents, and how much my parents love her. I had such a good time."

To make such a radical shift is possible when you arrive at therapy with the readiness to make the necessary change. It's not likely that Marilyn will always have such a good time with her parents, but this practice provided her an important window of opportunity she will be able to access in the future.

The Bottom-Line Issue

When SST therapists feel they have a reliable plan of action or simply see how to guide clients to their own conclusions, they should lead the session to its conclusion. Before closing a session I personally like to take a time-out to think everything over and reconvene a few minutes later. (Most therapists don't do this.) Before the break, I may say:

"You told me a lot of personal things about yourself, and I would like to go over everything you told me so that I give it all the necessary thought. Before we take a break, I wonder if there is anything we did not mention today, that you would like me to know about."

I'll also inquire:

"You have been very kind to answer all my questions. I'm wondering if you have any questions or requests for me."

In this way SST therapists try to convey that they value everything they have heard and that they take it seriously. Because therapy involves intimate matters, people often will hide the bottom-line issue until the last minute, as they walk out the therapist's door. When they are invited to add last-minute information, they may come up with some issue they were fearful about bringing up before. By giving a client a chance to be the one who raises the question, I often hear the bottom-line question that brought him or her to therapy. "Do you think you can help me? Is there any hope for me?" "Do you think I'm going crazy?" "Have I done the right thing. . . ?" "Should I take this step (get married, get divorced, leave home, take a job)?"

So before I take my break, I ask these last-minute questions to make sure we are on the same wavelength. I check by playing back what I hear to be the bottom-line concern, the purpose or question that brought the patient to see me today. "I understand that you want to know if the mood swings and poor self-image you've experienced since the divorce can be lifted." "If I understood you correctly you came here today because you are worried that your spouse is going crazy. Since he is unwilling to see a therapist, you wanted to check with me if your spouse is really becoming irrational."

The Take-Home Message

During the break I review my notes, gather my thoughts, and organize my concluding feedback. Memory is selective, and it is hard to know what clients will choose to remember from a SST. The final words are often what is remembered and the break serves further to emphasize this take-home message. In summarizing the session, the SST therapist may include the following elements:

1. Provide acknowledgment, understanding, and empathy: In the concluding statement, SST therapists try to put themselves in the client's shoes and express human understanding and appreciation for the long road the client has traveled and the underlying pain he or she has had to bear.

> *"It must have been difficult to keep it all inside for such a long time. It takes a lot of courage to open up about such a painful subject, as you have done today.*
>
> *"You have always given of yourself so devoutly and completely to others and yet you feel so undeserving and unappreciated."*

2. Emphasize strengths, abilities, and a helpful solution: When a person is demoralized and feels hopeless, as many

patients do, he or she tends to ignore the positive signs. When a therapist listens carefully to people's life stories, he or she soon realizes that no situation is totally bad and hopeless. Even people with the most severe problems and situations do some useful things some of the time. Every rule has an exception. In every disorder there is some order. Every human being has some redeeming qualities, abilities, and strengths. In the feedback, SST therapists pick up from the session all that they heard that the patient has done to move in the right direction. They pull out of the session all of those exceptions and play them back to the client with appropriate acknowledgment and appreciation.

I may say to the mother of a disturbed youngster:

"I was impressed by how much devotion and love you showed by your tireless efforts to help your son grow up. I noticed that he came here today even though he doesn't like psychologists or therapy. That shows me that you were able to communicate to him clearly how concerned you are about him and that you'll do whatever is necessary to help him get out of trouble."

SST therapists try to underline what the client is doing right, what steps the client is taking in the right direction. They express a genuine appreciation of the client's abilities and strengths and of the attempted solution as a way of returning the healing capacity to where it belongs: to the patient and her or his social support system.

3. Reframe the problem: In order to offer hope and reliable solutions, therapists need to offer the client a way of viewing the problem itself as a source of hope, self-mastery,

or at least as a valuable challenge. A therapist should not hand down a verdict from on high. The therapist needs to challenge the client to change. He or she needs to give the client hope that such change is possible. By reframing the problem in positive or surprising new terms, therapists try to capture the listener's ear and lead to new possibilities for handling the problem.

For example, a therapist may suggest that a client view anxiety attacks as a clear signal that he or she needs to make some changes in lifestyle. A therapist may reframe depression as an act of love and care or as a challenge to be kinder and more true to her or his basic needs. A therapist may suggest that terrible guilt feelings about past mistakes indicate that the client replaced a required action with a bad feeling.

Therapy, like life, is an adventure in forgiveness. People need to forgive themselves and those who hurt them and move on with life. They need to stop doing something that isn't working anymore. When I reframe a problem, I try to give my client back both autonomy and hope. If I have no good news to tell, I like to introduce a challenge or humor instead. I try to avoid medical or psychiatric labels unless medications are required. (These medications are required only in a small minority of cases.)

I try not to add any moral judgment of my own. For example, although I hate seeing parents hit children, I may relabel the hitting this way:

"I realize how much you want to educate your child, so he will have a brighter and better future than your own."

I personally will always believe that hitting a child is a crime. Yet, I don't see myself as judging or policing my clients. My job is to be an effective facilitator of change. The best way to change people is to get them to cooperate in doing what is within their capabilities and best interests. I do this by discussing their problems within the context of their values and philosophies.

4. Suggest a take-home task: In the closing statement the SST therapist suggests some task to enhance the changes that were explored during the session. I personally tend to give simple tasks that do more of what's working and do less of what doesn't work. The SST therapist gives tasks that interrupt destructive behavior or disturbing thoughts. I'll suggest that the patient do more of what seems to work well, such as taking breaks, initiating joyful activities, or taking time to talk more with a supportive friend.

5. Leave an open door for further changes: When you are debating whether to come back for more therapy, the SST therapist stresses that the choice is between a few more sessions, ongoing therapy, or ad hoc therapy—an open door to come back whenever necessary. Life is full of changes and challenges and things are never fixed once and for all. If, for example, you feel at the end of SST that you have accomplished what you wanted for now, the SST therapist will suggest that you call him or her in a month and talk about how things are progressing. Otherwise, the SST therapist should call you in three months for a routine follow-up to assess the results of the SST.

I saw Carol for SST with hypnotherapy for smoking cessation. At the end of the session she was asked if she wished to make another appointment or if she wanted to leave herself an open door to return whenever necessary. She replied: "Let me first see how it is working with everyday temptations and stresses. If it works, fine. If not, I can always call you back."

"That's right. I think after SST it is good to let things filter down and be absorbed. Call me after three or four weeks, but no longer than two months, to let me know how things are going. If I don't hear from you, I'll call you myself in three months to hear how you're doing."

When Carol called after a month to report a total absence of smoking, I challenged her by raising questions about relapse and possible symptoms resulting from the physical addiction to nicotine in hopes of preventing relapse. Carol expressed confidence in her ability and I reaffirmed my availability on an as-needed basis. At a one-year follow-up she was not smoking and reported further gains and changes in her lifestyle.

At the very end of SST, a client needs to reaffirm the commitment to action and change. Sharon had a very intrusive and toxic father. Before closing the session my colleague in the SST research asked her, "What are you actually going to do when this meeting is over?"

Sharon replied, "Draw a line. Draw a line!"

"How and where are you going to draw the line?" the therapist asked.

"I will start with the phone calls, because that is how I'll hear from him next."

The therapist then asked, "And what are you going to do?"

Sharon answered loud and firm, "Not accept the next call!"

"Perfect!" said the therapist. "Let's shake hands on that."

Even though life may seem perfect and encouraging at the end of a good SST, events and feelings may end up unfolding in ways that will keep people feeling stuck. In such cases a client may need a few more sessions to complete therapy successfully and sufficiently. If this is necessary, read on to the next chapter.

When More Is Better
(or Necessary)

SST is common and can be very helpful, but one session may not suffice for every problem or everybody. Often a client may need a few more sessions to take hold of a problem, to make sure the change is lasting, or to handle a relapse of the problem. It is not therapeutic, in any length of therapy, to feel abandoned or short-changed. The optimal length of therapy is the one that matches the client's expectations and needs. The therapist may try to sell the idea that a client's needs are much greater than he or she realizes. Every good salesperson would do the same, but hopefully he or she would first listen to the client so that what is sold is really needed and not the most expensive item in the store. The process of matching expectations and needs to the appropriate length and method of therapy is a critical step. For example, you cannot expect in a single session of therapy to fully recover from the horror of repeated sexual abuse by your parent. You will be the first person to know when you have had enough. The decisions about when to start and when to end therapy should always rest with you, the client. You may not know in advance if you need only one or five sessions, but you know that for most people, in most conditions (probably including conditions worse than yours), one or very few sessions can be sufficient.

When a Few More Sessions Are Necessary

Remember that therapy should be helpful, appropriate, and effective. There is nothing wrong with taking a few extra sessions to reach some satisfactory and positive closure to the therapeutic process.

SST is an approach to therapy and not a single technique or unified method. There are many good ways to conduct brief, effective therapy. In the following pages I'll describe a partial list of other methods of therapy, all of which attempt to make therapy as brief as possible. All are well established with thousands of trained therapists throughout the United States and were originated by innovative therapists I admire and who influenced my development as a therapist. I'll also describe here other methods of brief therapy developed by other therapists who work in an approach similar to the one presented in this book. These are therapists who treat most problems within ten sessions or less. If you like the idea of therapy being as brief as possible, but feel you need a few more sessions, read on.

Ericksonian Approaches to Brief Therapy

Most brief therapists were influenced in some way by the work of the late Milton H. Erickson, M.D. He practiced therapy in Phoenix, Arizona, from the late 1920s until the late 1970s, a period when most therapists considered long-term therapy the only acceptable way of doing therapy, and psychoanalysis was considered mainstream. He was so versatile and flexible in his methods of helping people change that his followers are all distinctly different from one another, yet all are able to claim they use Ericksonian methods. Erickson can be considered a brief or even a single-session therapist, since he treated many cases within one or a few sessions. Yet he had patients who saw him daily for many years and he can therefore be considered a long-term therapist as well. Erickson simply hated to be labeled or limited by any one approach or method. He used whatever worked! He had no unified theory, only hundreds of creative, almost genius "tricks" to make people change, especially in turning what seemed like liabilities into assets. For example, when he treated a young man with very little self-esteem who had just obtained a job in a bank, he took particular interest in mistakes the young man had made in his new job. Erickson described the case: "Every time he made a mistake in his work, what interested me *always* was the procedure by which it was corrected—never the details of how he made the error." By paying attention to the young man's corrections, Erickson was using the mistakes as a way to help him build his self-confidence. (This is described in *Conversations with Milton H. Erickson* edited by Jay Haley.)

Ericksonian methods often use hypnosis during the sessions and tasks for after the session, all of which aim to arrange circumstances that permit clients to make their own appropriate choices. These are often particular tasks that may seem unconnnected to the problem to help the client learn through his or her own efforts; they may be specific, physical experiences like climbing a mountain. There are more than one hundred books on Erickson and Ericksonian methods of psychotherapy and hypnotherapy, written mostly for therapists. There are more than fifty institutes and many therapists throughout the world who conduct and teach Ericksonian psychotherapy and hypnotherapy.

To find one near you, call or write to:
The Milton H. Erickson Foundation
3606 N. 24th Street
Phoenix, AZ 85016-6500
Tel: (602) 956-6196

RECOMMENDED READINGS:

1. Sidney Rosen, ed. *My Voice Will Go with You: The Teaching Tales of Milton H. Erickson.* New York: W. W. Norton, 1982.
2. Haley, J. *Uncommon Therapy: The Psychiatric Techniques of Milton H. Erickson, M.D.* New York: W. W. Norton, 1973.
3. *An Uncommon Case Book: The Complete Clinical Work of Milton H. Erickson, M.D.* Summarized and compiled by William Hudson O'Hanlon and Angela L. Hexum, New York: W. W. Norton, 1990.

Solution-Focused Therapy

Solution-focused brief therapy is a method that was developed during the 1980s by a group of therapists in Milwaukee, Wisconsin, led by Steve de Shazer. With the average of six sessions they successfully treated difficult problems such as depression, marital conflicts, substance abuse, violence, and sexual abuse. In this approach clients and therapists talk very little about the nature of the problem or the history of the client or his or her family. They talk in great detail about present and future solutions. They use a simple, straightforward method of interviewing clients and giving them simple tasks at the end of the session. The tasks are similar to the ones suggested in this book, requiring that clients make observations or do something new in their own lives or in their relationships with others. Unlike Erickson they use no hypnosis and no complex methods. They emphasize cooperation, simplicity, and practicality.

In the first session, regardless of the presented problem, they tend to present the "exception question" and the "miracle question" and assign at the end of the session "the first session task." The exception question directs clients to search for times when they did not or have not had their problems even when they expected they would. For example, when a client complains about feeling anxious, he or she may be asked, "What is different about the times when you are less anxious?" Every problem, even the most severe ones, has exceptions. By focusing on exceptions, client and therapist may discover solutions that they had forgotten about.

While the exception question directs the client to search in the present and the past, the miracle question prompts him or her to look forward to the future. The miracle question is: "Suppose that one night, while you were asleep, there was a miracle and this problem was solved. How would you know? What would be different?" The miracle question tries to make a better future more tangible and helps the therapist find clues toward which to direct the client. For example, if the client answers that after such a miracle he or she will take more nature trips, the therapist may prescribe taking one such trip before the next session. So in this way the client makes his or her future vision into today's reality.

If a client is less committed and active, the solution-focused therapist prescribes only an observation task which is spelled out by Steve de Shazer of the Brief Therapy Center in Milwaukee,

Wisconsin: "Between now and the next time we meet, I would like you to carefully observe so you can describe to me next time what happens in your family/life/marriage/relationship that you want to continue to have happen."

This simple task seems to help with a wide range of problems. A few years ago I was advised by a colleague to try this task with an AIDS patient I treated. How in the world can such a simple task help with such terminal and devastating illness? I thought to myself. My patient had a very short time left to live. He was isolated, depressed, and weak. I gave him the task simply because I didn't know anything else I could do or say. It did him so much good that it became our standard task for the rest of the sessions (and his life). He was able to report to me every week about the things he wanted to keep happening in his life while living with a lot of pain, in a grave situation. He became incredibly skilled at identifying even the most minute pleasures.

The Milwaukee research team did a follow-up survey of this task. Fifty out of fifty-six clients reported noticing things they wanted to continue and forty-six of the fifty described at least one of these things as something they hadn't noticed before.

Training and therapy in this method is provided at:

The Brief Family Therapy Center (they treat individuals and couples)
6815 West Capitol Drive
Milwaukee, WI 53216
Tel: (414) 464-7775

Hundreds of therapists in the United States, Canada, Europe, and the Pacific Rim were trained by this group. You can obtain a recommendation for a therapist near you by calling the above center.

RECOMMENDED READINGS:

1. de Shazer, S. *Keys to Solutions in Brief Therapy.* New York: W. W. Norton, 1985.
2. O'Hanlon, W. H., and M. Weiner-Davis. *In Search of Solutions.* New York: W. W. Norton, 1989.
3. Berg, I., and S. Miller. *Working with the Problem Drinker.* New York: W. W. Norton, 1993.

Strategic Brief Therapy

Strategic brief therapy started in 1966 when a chemical engineer-turned-family therapist (John Weakland), a psychiatrist (Richard Fisch), and a psychologist (Paul Watzlawick) began a brief therapy project in the Mental Research Institute (MRI) in Palo Alto, California. (This method is also known as problem-solving therapy or the MRI model.) They worked within a deliberate time limit of ten sessions treating problems that are usually associated with very lengthy therapy such as schizophrenia and anorexia-bulimia. Jay Haley, a former team member of MRI, moved to the East Coast and founded, with Cloe Madanes, the Family Therapy Institute of Washington, D.C. Haley and Madanes have written extensively on this model, particularly regarding working with families with disturbed youngsters. The main principle of their work is to focus on the presented problem rather than try to reorganize families or develop deep insights. Problems are viewed to be interactional in nature. Thus, when a person experiences a problem, it is not viewed as if it were "all in the head," a flaw etched in a person's character, or a sign of mental illness. Instead, problems are a result of unsuccessful attempts to solve them. Problems consist basically of a vicious cycle where some behavior gets labeled as wrong or inappropriate, which leads to efforts to get rid of the behavior. The treatment aim is to interrupt the vicious cycle that maintains the behavior, most often by creating a convincing rationale to stop the repeated attempts at the same solution.

Paul Watzlawick and others, in their book *Change: Principles of Problem Formation and Problem Resolution,* tell of a family who sought therapy because the father/husband appeared depressed. His wife and other family members tried their utmost to cheer him up. When their efforts failed they tried even harder to make him think positively. This, again, only seemed to make matters worse. The therapist told the wife that her husband did seem depressed and that his family obviously cared a great deal about him and his welfare. All the steps they had taken thus far to help him feel better were obvious signs of that love and caring. However, they were told, there might be one thing that they hadn't thought of which could demonstrate their love for him even more.

The therapist proceeded to explain that he thought the father felt misunderstood, that no one could really appreciate his devastation. After all, if they really understood, how could they say simply, "cheer up?"

"What he really needs right now," suggested the therapist, "is to feel that you are really with him. You can do this by agreeing with him when he complains about things. You can also help him feel closer to you by occasionally talking about things which get you down too. This will help him feel less isolated." Once the family stopped trying to cheer him up, his depression was lifted.

The method used here and in other cases of this model is called "reframing." The therapist uses the "frame of mind," the belief system of his or her clients, but gives them a new angle, a new frame of reference, which allows them to act or think differently. Problem-solving therapy is strategic, highly pragmatic, and behavioral. This type of therapy is most appropriate for families and couples, and less so with individuals who seek insights or view their problems as personal ones.

RECOMMENDED READINGS:

1. Haley, J. *Problem-Solving Therapy.* 2d ed. San Francisco: Jossey-Bass, 1987.
2. Rabkin, R. *Strategic Psychotherapy: Brief and Symptomatic Treatment.* New York: Basic Books, 1977.
3. Fisch, R., J. H. Weakland, L. Segal. *The Tactics of Change: Doing Therapy Briefly.* San Francisco: Jossey-Bass, 1983.

For more information about a brief, strategic therapist near you, contact:

The Brief Therapy Center
Mental Research Institute
555 Middlefield Road
Palo Alto, CA 94301
Tel: (415) 321-3055

or:

Family Therapy Institute of Washington, D. C.
5850 Hubbard Drive
Georgetown Park
Rockville, MD 20852
Tel: (301) 984-5730

Brief Behavior Therapy: Francine Shapiro's EMDR

At times the most innovative treatments are discovered accidentally. This is the case with psychologist Francine Shapiro who in

1987 discovered that disturbing thoughts lost much of their power when the person engaged in a particular kind of repeated saccadic eye movement. As a result Shapiro developed eye movement desensitization and reprocessing procedure, or EMDR, which was found to be an effective and rapid treatment modality for anxiety and trauma victims (in cases, for example, of rape, war, and abuse). Within one to four sessions, clients experienced significant reductions in symptoms like nightmares, intrusive thoughts, flashbacks, and anxiety. The improvements were maintained when follow-up was conducted three months later.

The procedure is quite simple:

1. The client and therapist identify the symptoms of the problem as well as the desired positive self-assessment.
2. The client is asked to maintain in his or her awareness an image of the traumatic memory and/or the physical sensations that accompany the anxiety response.
3. Simultaneously, the therapist induces a variety of repetitive eye movements by asking the client to follow a repeated simple movement of the therapist's finger.

The advantage of behavioral procedures like the eye movement is that it is a standardized technique that requires little time, expense, or risks. It gives clients a ritual to replace a negative feeling (like anxiety) or intrusive thoughts (like flashbacks of a traumatic scene), with a more positive, balanced, and calm experience. It seems to work due to some combination of scientific processes in the brain and the belief in the ritual itself to create a bridge from the problem to the solution. Like any other therapeutic technique, it will work with only some problems, some of the time, although Shapiro claims it can be used to deal with any dysfunctional emotion, and that it can also enhance positive states of mind.

To illustrate when it can be useful, Shapiro provided the following examples. Two children witnessed the horrific death of a parent and experienced extreme grief, rage, and guilt. When remembering the late parent, they had only memories of the death circumstances. Immediately after the EMDR procedure was conducted, pleasurable memories of the parent resurfaced.

A woman who was an adult child of an alcoholic requested treatment for anxiety and a high level of interpersonal and social dysfunction. Specific anxiety-producing situations from her past and present life were isolated in the initial session. In the next few sessions the EMDR procedure desensitized all of these anxiety-producing traumas. Simultaneously, positive cognition and beliefs were suggested. For example, when she was asked to imagine interacting with her husband and to get in touch with the anxiety that the interaction produced, she reported seeing herself as child-sized, with her husband towering over her. During the repeated sets of eye movements, she reported seeing herself spontaneously "growing" and experiencing less and less anxiety, until the imagery presented itself to her mind with her and her spouse standing eye to eye. She was then asked to imagine herself interacting with him easily and comfortably. She reported feeling progressively more "empowered" as the eye movements were continued. At the next session she reported that "something had shifted" and she was able to interact with her husband "as an equal" and with no distress.

Shapiro's procedure with this case as well as with Vietnam vets and rape victims exemplifies that complex problems do not necessarily require lengthy and expensive solutions. She posits that there is an innate information processing system that is hardwired—not just psychological, but fundamentally neurological. The information from the trauma is locked in the nervous system in its original disturbing form. The eye movements may assist in catalyzing the information-processing system and transforming the information into some resolution. Follow-up interviews three years after brief EMDR treatment indicate that the positive effects of the treatment were maintained.

In the last few years Shapiro has provided extensive training to thousands of therapists, who are now qualified to use EMDR. Shapiro warns that you need to use only trained therapists in this method to ensure efficacy and client safety.

For a referral or further information contact:
    Francine Shapiro, Ph.D.
    or Robbie Dunton, Coordinator
    EMDR
    PO Box 51010
    Pacific Grove, CA 93950-6010
    Tel: (408) 372-3900
    Fax: (408) 647-9881

Cognitive-Behavioral Therapy

Cognitive-behavioral therapy (CBT) is an amalgam of empirically established techniques and procedures drawn from both cognitive and behavioral research. Most therapists who previously were identified as either cognitive or behavioral therapists have merged into one school of therapy called cognitive-behavioral therapy. A recent review lists eighteen cognitive techniques and nine behavioral techniques commonly practiced by CB therapists. CBT is a structured and comprehensive approach that emphasizes teaching of certain cognitive and behavioral skills. For example, it will teach you how to replace depressive thoughts ("It's all my fault," "It's never going to work"), with a more balanced yet optimistic view of yourself and the world ("Not everything is my fault," "It did not work out today, but I may have another chance tomorrow"). Such a process may (or may not) be brief. On the average it requires eight sessions but may vary quite a bit. The three basic assumptions of CBT are:

1. How people think impels their behavior and emotions in critically important ways. When people change how they think, their actions and feelings will follow.

2. People learn most of their destructive behaviors and thoughts; therefore they can unlearn or relearn them. For example, you can learn to be an optimist, you can learn to appreciate and like yourself regardless of a highly negative upbringing.

3. What matters is not what happens in life but how people take it in. People see what they want to see. They hear what they are prepared to hear and this is usually a partial, even distorted version of the reality.

CBT is a collaborative effort of client and therapist to identify assumptions of the world, attribution style (the way in which people take responsibility for events that happen to them), and habitual, automatic thoughts. Once these are identified, the therapist will challenge the client to develop alternative understandings of day-to-day events, develop more flexible and optimistic assumptions about the world, and finally, rehearse cognitive and behavioral responses based on these new assumptions.

Here is a conversation between a CB therapist and a depressed woman who wants to end her life. It represents a typical CBT exchange.

Therapist (T): Why do you want to end your life?

Client (C): Without Raymond [her husband], I am nothing. I can't be happy without Raymond. But I can't save our marriage.

T: What has your marriage been like?

C: It has been miserable from the very beginning. Raymond has always been unfaithful. I have hardly seen him in the past five years.

T: You say that you can't be happy without Raymond. Have you found yourself happy when you are with Raymond?

C: No, we fight all the time and I feel worse.

T: You say you are nothing without Raymond. Before you met Raymond, did you feel you were nothing?

C: No, I felt I was somebody.

T: If you were somebody before you knew Raymond, why do you need him to be somebody now?

C: (puzzled) Hmmmm.

T: Did you have male friends before you knew Raymond?

C: I was pretty popular then.

T: Why do you think you will be unpopular without Raymond now?

C: Because I'll not be able to attract any other men.

T: Have any men shown an interest in you since you have been married?

C:	A lot of men have made passes at me, but I ignore them.
T:	If you were free of the marriage, do you think that men might be interested in you, knowing that you were available?
C:	I guess that maybe they would be.
T:	Is it possible that you might find a man who would be more constant than Raymond?
C:	I don't know. I guess it's possible.
T:	You say that you can't stand the idea of losing the marriage. Is it correct that you have hardly seen your husband in the past five years?
C:	That's right. I only see him a couple of times a year.
T:	Is there any chance of your getting back together with him?
C:	No. He has another woman. He doesn't want me.
T:	Then what have you actually lost if you break up the marriage?
C:	I don't know.
T:	Is it possible that you'll get along better if you end the marriage?
C:	There is no guarantee of that.
T:	Do you have a real marriage?
C:	I guess not.
T:	If you don't have a real marriage, what do you actually lose if you decide to end the marriage?
C:	(long pause) Nothing, I guess.

The therapist in this case was Aaron Beck, M.D., who developed the cognitive therapy during the 1970s at the University of

Pennsylvania Medical School. The therapist here is quite active and direct, and constantly challenges the patient's assumptions and conclusions about the problem by raising detailed questions that encourage the patient to rethink and reexamine the issues. More recently, CBT methods were applied not just to depression-related scenarios but also to more complicated problems such as personality and marital difficulties.

What I particularly like about CBT is its solid and extensive research base. Using well-designed studies, researchers compared it with other methods of treatment such as antidepressant medications, insight therapy, supportive therapy, relaxation training, and non-directive therapy. It was consistently found to be as effective or more effective than these other methods. It is particularly helpful with depression and anxiety, but in the last ten years has been used effectively in many other personal and interpersonal problems. Several of its leaders have successfully translated the method into popular self-help books, a few of which are listed here.

RECOMMENDED READINGS:
1. Burns, D. *Feeling Good: The New Mood Therapy.* New York: Signet, 1980.
2. Beck, A. *Love is Never Enough.* New York: Harper & Row, 1988.
3. Seligman, M. E. P. *Learned Optimism: How to Change Your Mind and Your Life.* Alfred A. Knopf, 1990.

For national referral service write or call:
Center for Cognitive Therapy
University of Pennsylvania, Rm 754, Science Center
3600 Market St.
Philadelphia, PA 19104-2648
Tel: (215) 898-4100

Association for Advancement of Behavior Therapy
15 W. 36th Street, 9th floor
New York, NY 10018
Tel: (212) 279-7970

Institute for Rational-Emotive Therapy
45 E. 65th Street
New York, NY 10021
Tel: (212) 535-0822

Neuro-Linguistic Programming (NLP)

NLP is an elaborate and specific set of methods for creating rapid change and quick problem solving. It was originally developed in the 1970s by Richard Bandler and John Grinder who carefully analyzed the therapeutic work of two widely acknowledged "master" therapists: a family therapist named Virginia Satir and hypnotist Milton Erickson. From this they developed step-by-step, standardized procedures or "recipes" for treating different kinds of problems. It is not as extensively researched as CBT but clinically it is quite rich and full of promise.

The basic assumption of NLP is that all experiences—memories, plans, hopes, fears, and decisions—are composed of the building blocks of sensory experience, the five senses: sight, sound, feeling, smell, and taste. The five senses are composed of smaller elements, called submodalities. For instance, a visual image can be large or small, near or far, in color or black and white. Typically, if you evoke an image that is large, close, and in color it will elicit a much stronger response than one that is small, distant, and in black and white. NLP identifies the senses and submodalities of a problem or experience using verbal and non-verbal cues, and then works to alter it. NLP teaches simple exercises to use in order to shift and change how the client experiences the problem. For instance, taking a troublesome memory, and working on making the image small, distant, and gray, allowing the sound and color to drain out of it, will make the memory much less troublesome. It is quite common for NLP therapists to treat a problem in one or a few sessions. It is best suited to well-defined and well-targeted problems. For example, Lori was treated in one session to cure a severe bee phobia she'd had for twenty years. When she was 11 years old, she fell into a wasps' nest and was stung hundreds of times. Since then, as she put it, "When a bee is in the house, I'm not!"

After the therapist (Steve Andreas) established contact with Lori, he was able to observe her phobic reactions by asking her to imagine a bee in the room with her. Then, he got her back to a normal, relaxed state and started the intervention. First, he asked her to imagine being in a movie theater. Once she was able to do that, the therapist guided her.

Therapist (T): Now I want you to leave that black and white movie that's on the screen, and I want you to float out of your body that's sitting here in the chair, up to the projection booth of the movie theater. Can you do that? Take a little while . . .

Lori (L): O.K.

T: So you can kind of see through the glass, and there are holes in the glass so you can hear the movie, because we're going to show a movie pretty soon. What I want you to do is run a movie of yourself in one of those traumatic times when you used to respond to that particular thing. And run it from beginning to end, and stay back in that projection booth . . . . See yourself freaking out over there in response to one of those situations. That's right. Take all the time you need, and just let me know when you got to the end.

L: It's hard to get to the end.

T: O.K. What makes it difficult?

L: It just seems to stop . . . . The particular incident goes over and over and over and doesn't seem to have an end, although I know it ended.

The therapist suggests that Lori speed it up so she can see it over and over again, and asks her how many times it has to go over and over before she can get to the end.

L: Umm, half a dozen.

T: O.K. So let it flip through half a dozen repetitions, so it'll let you get to the end . . . . And when I say "end" I mean after the whole thing is finished and you're back to normal again.

After the therapist confirmed that she was able to get to the end, Lori conveyed that she felt "a little uncomfortable, but not bad. Not like the real thing." The therapist then moved to the next stage where he asked Lori to get out of the projection booth and out of the audience chair and imagine herself inside the movie at the very end. He asked her to run it backwards in color, to be inside "so it's just like you're really there." He guided her to go through the experience backwards, several times and very fast. At the end of the process, the therapist tested her response by asking her to imagine a bee again.

177

T: Now let's make it a real bad one, you know. Have a bee come in and land on your hand or something. (Lori looks down at her hand.) Can you imagine that?

Lori shakes her head in disbelief as she calmly describes to the therapist the feeling of the bee sitting directly on her hand. There is a big difference between the previous test and the relative ease she feels now.

A year later, the therapist took a jar with about a dozen honeybees to Lori's house. She comfortably held the jar with the bees and examined them closely. The therapist let a few bees out of the jar and Lori watched them crawling on her living room window without any reactions. A bee was in her house, and this time, so was she. Eight years later, Lori is still free of her old phobia.

In this case, as in many NLP, visual imagery, EMDR, and hypnotherapy cases, the procedure is to dissociate the client from the traumatic experience. A vivid experiential technique allows a client to dissociate himself or herself from the traumatic memory and develop an alternate experience. In the above case, it was first done from the safety of the projection booth, later from the audience chair. Once able to visualize a positive normal ending, Lori was asked to view it from the inside, but backwards. The procedure is gradual yet vivid, allowing the client to experience an immediate change and check the results *in vivo* at a follow-up session (in this case a year later).

At times, NLP seems to promise more than it can deliver. It may appeal to clients who want "to go to sleep and wake up without the problem." The therapist does most of the guiding by following the client's verbal and non-verbal responses.

NLP puts a lot of emphasis on patterns or "recipes." What is similar between NLP and SST is the expectation that within the first one to three sessions, clients should be able to experience significant progress toward the changes they want. "If they don't," said Andreas, "we advise them to try some other approach . . . . We accomplish what we can in the first session—which may run to two or three hours if needed—with follow-up sessions as desired or indicated." (The above case and the description of NLP therapy is taken from *Heart of the Mind,* by Steve Andreas and Connaire Andreas [1989].)

RECOMMENDED READINGS:
1. Bandler, R. *Using Your Brain—for a Change.* Moab, UT: Real People Press, 1985.
2. Andreas, C., and S. Andreas. *Heart of the Mind.* Moab, UT: Real People Press, 1989.

For national referral service:
North American Association of Neuro-Linguistic Programming
8335 Allison Pointe Trail, Suite 250
Indianapolis, IN 46250
Tel: (317) 841-8038

Mann's Time-Limited Psychodynamic Therapy

One of the guiding principles of in-depth, insight therapy is to provide an open-ended, time-unlimited therapy to allow for the building of trust and the ability to free-associate and experience extreme emotions safely; to explore the tricky inroads of the unconscious and face basic human conflicts. Most psychoanalytic and psychodynamic approaches advocate open-ended therapy. Over the last twenty years, a dozen leading therapists within this school started to challenge the notion that in-depth therapy must be time-unlimited. One of them is James Mann of Boston University School of Medicine, who, during the 1970s, suggested therapy should be limited to twelve treatment hours with a fixed ending date agreed to in advance by both therapist and client. Mann argued in his book, *The Time-Limited Psychotherapy,* that time-unlimited, long-term therapy "leads to a steady widening of and diffusion of content. This creates a growing sense of ambiguity in the mind of the therapist as to what he is about, and . . . it surely increases the patient's dependence on the therapist. The result is that patient and therapist come to need each other, so that bringing the case to a conclusion seems impossible."

What is special about Mann's approach, in addition to the pre-set length, is the insistence that core, deep conflicts from a person's past can be sufficiently treated within twelve sessions. Mann draws heavily on psychoanalytic theories of personality and psychopathology. His therapeutic focus on pathology, the past, and insoluble psychological conflicts is very different from the other approaches presented in this book. What is similar is the attempt to create a central focused theme in the first session. In the very first session Mann tries to identify a central unresolved issue that leads to chronic, underlying enduring pain. He has identified four central psychological dilemmas (or conflicts): independence versus dependence, activity versus passivity, adequate self-esteem versus diminished or lost self-esteem, and unresolved or delayed grief resulting from an earlier separation.

Mann tries at the end of the initial session to connect empathetically with the client enduring pain. An example of expressing a central theme could be, "You have always feared that despite your best efforts you will lose everything." Mann found that after the first session, once a patient opened up and a central theme was identified, many clients experienced rapid symptomatic improvement and substantial relief. During the middle phase of the twelve sessions, according to Mann, clients are bound to experience some setback as old hurts are revived. Mann uses this phase to help the client gain insight into the deep feelings of separation anxiety and strong dependency needs toward the therapist. During the final phase of treatment, the client's reaction to termination becomes the focus of discussion. Like other psychoanalytical therapists, Mann believes that separation from the therapist stands in direct symbolic relationship with all previous losses and separation, and resolution of this separation is the key to the therapeutic effect.

It may give you a good flavor of what transpires in Mann's therapy when you see how he handles the ending of his pre-set time-limited therapy. This sample case is that of a married 32-year-old special education teacher who was forced to take a leave from his job after developing extreme anxiety when he was assigned to a class consisting of five disturbed children. The classroom provoked rapid heartbeat, perspiration, a knot in his stomach, and a sense of dread. Being left alone to handle aggressive, uncontrolled children triggered what Mann identified as a central theme: "You have long been plagued by the fear of helplessness if you are left alone." This fear was worked on for most of the twelve sessions, particularly in regard to the patient's sense of loss of a guiding parental figure.

Here is how Mann handled the termination of the twelve-session therapy and dealt with the client's need for his "parental approval," as reported in *A Casebook in Time-Limited Psychotherapy.*

Client (C):   I'm aware that maybe I'm warding off other feelings but I do feel that rather than this being only a termination, for me, it is a beginning—a new world of options has been opened to me that I never knew before.

Therapist (T): I agree with you. Nevertheless, you might be avoiding other feelings. You may feel depressed or angry in the next days and if you do it will have to do with feelings about me.

C: I realize that your approval of me has become important.

T: Do you like me?

C: I really do.

T: Then you may feel that since you worked so hard for me, why am I sending you away, why am I leaving you?

C: I know that I have made great gains and I know, too, that you may have better patients.

T: Shall I give you an A-plus?

C: I'm really satisfied with a C.

T: But you see that there is the hint again of your wish for my approval.

C: You know, I've had the feeling of instant cure. I'm suspicious of that.

T: You are not cured. You will run up against these problems again but you will know what they are about and be able to handle them.

C: What seemed so far in the future when we started —termination—is now here.

T: I warn you again that you may feel depressed, or angry, or both, and it will have to do with feelings about me.

C: I think I'm in control. I feel that way, and I'll handle it. (Therapist and client say good-bye.)

Unlike the SST therapist, Mann's main therapeutic tools are the transference feelings and the expectations the client projects onto the therapist. What is similar is the acknowledgment that therapy will take exactly the time allocated for it. Mann makes his client acutely aware of the passage of time and the unavoidable acceptance that everything in life comes to an end. Therapy must continue outside of the session, and change will continue once therapy is terminated. Mann does not promise a cure but prepares his client for the hardships of separation. He promises less and delivers more. For example, he says good-bye and makes no further promise to stay in touch or be available to his clients. Yet, without prior indication of his intent to do so, Mann systematically uses follow-up interviews as a way of collecting information on the vicissitudes of the therapeutic process after its formal conclusion. This follow-up is an excellent way of accomplishing two objectives at the same time—enhancing the therapeutic effects while simultaneously enhancing clients' and therapists' understanding of the therapeutic process.

I also conduct follow-ups with my SST clients, though I tell them I will do so in advance. I am always learning something new by encouraging my clients to review their own progress. I often gain a new perspective as a result of the time that has elapsed between the session and the follow-ups, and the questions we discussed in the follow-up call, such as:

• What do you think made the change possible?
• What else has changed since our last session?

- What other people around you notice or comment about your changes?
- What would you do in case of a relapse or setback?

Unlike Mann, my experience has been that clients call me (or come to see me) less often when they trust that I'm there whenever necessary and that my door is open. A follow-up phone call reestablishes this knowledge and fulfills that promise. Only in a minority of cases do I learn in the follow-up that my client "fell between the cracks" or that nothing had changed for the better. In such cases the follow-up is used to reinstate therapy or to propose a possible, better alternative if the client did not like me or felt that therapy was not the answer to his or her problems.

For further reading on eleven other brief methods of psychoanalytic and psychodynamic therapy, you can read the second section in:

1. Bloom, B. *Planned Short-Term Psychotherapy*. Needham Heights, MA: Allyn and Bacon, 1992.

About Mann's method you can read:

2. Mann, J. *The Time-Limited Psychotherapy*. Cambridge, MA: Harvard University Press, 1973.

3. Mann, J., and R. Goldman. *A Casebook in Time-Limited Psychotherapy*. New York: McGraw-Hill, 1982.

Going Back to Therapy?

Once you have terminated therapy, what if you got "stuck" again with the same (or a new) problem? "I'm having the blues again. Should I go to see the therapist again?" "We had an ugly fight last night. Do we need to see somebody?"

The truth is, life often feels like one crisis after another, and almost every day it would be nice to consult a wise person or simply have a sounding board to bounce things off of. If you benefited from seeing a therapist, going back will seem even easier than going the first time. A conventional therapist will tell you, "If you are not sure, why don't you go and see someone, check it out with your therapist." My approach is that you should go only when it is absolutely necessary. You want to know that help is available and accessible. Yet, this sense should provide you with a safety net for emergencies rather than a crutch for everyday problems.

I had seen Jeremy two years earlier for an SST. When he called to say "I want to come in," I asked, "Why now?"

"You may be surprised to hear it," he replied, "but I still remember what you told me two years ago. I guess I was not ready at the time to really do anything about it. The situation has gotten so bad now that I have no other choice but to get my act together."

You may need to reach the "end of your rope" in order to be mentally ready to change habits in drinking, diets, drugs, or intimate relationships. Before you go back to therapy, you should check in with your "natural co-therapist." We often bypass our best allies: a spouse, a friend, and family members who can help us better than any therapist.

Reasons to Seek Long-Term Therapy

What about therapy as a long road instead of as a turning point? Undoubtedly there are legitimate reasons to seek long-term therapy. Therapy may last longer because you're dealing with a severe or complex problem, or you wish to learn skills you never had, which may require a long process of apprenticeship. Remember, though, that there is no standard or correct correlation between severity of problem and length of therapy; the main variables are readiness, timing, and expectation. The length of therapy is a matter of expectation and the way you define your purpose in therapy. Here are a few common ways by which you convey (although you may not have intended to do so) your desire for a longer-term therapy.

- You want your therapist to become your companion or close adviser. You want to build a "substitute relationship" for a missing figure in your life. You are lonely. You want the therapist to hold your hand, be by your side throughout a lengthy process or stage in your life, be a friend and provide consistency, warmth, and availability—things you don't have enough of in relationships outside of therapy. You can secure this relationship by buying his or her services.
- You do not expect changes soon because the problem seems too diffuse or too complicated.
- You have vague complaints and general goals, such as "I don't like myself," or "I just want to have inner peace."
- During the first few sessions, you are unable to identify anything that works right for you. You are unable to acknowledge any strengths and abilities you have or you are unable to find anybody else who cares or wants to help with the problem. You need more time to build your self-esteem and learn optimism.
- You want therapy to be part of your weekly routine, like mental massage or exercise.
- You just want to understand *why* you do certain things. You want to achieve personal growth or explore "blind spots" in your personality.
- You previously saw a therapist for long-term therapy and grew accustomed to it. You now want (or feel you need) more of it.

- Your condition requires a combination of medication, surgery, and supportive therapy. Your problems stem from a medical or psychiatric condition that will not improve without medical intervention (as in manic-depression or cancer).

At times, even though you may not intend to spend a long time in therapy, you set yourself up by the way you describe your problem or goals in therapy. Watch your words! You are going to get what you ask for.

Here are a few common phrases or opening statements which serve as cues for long-term therapy:

"I want to understand the meaning/purpose of my life."
Most of these existential or philosophical dilemmas invite lengthy exploration. The psychological dilemmas that start with the word "why" are the bread and butter of long-term therapists, and it's relatively easy to find a therapist interested in joining you on such a journey. You may want to find out why you are the way you are. You may want to know why you get scared and pull out of a relationship when it gets intimate or serious. When you present your goal in therapy this way, you invite what therapists call "insight therapy." An insight therapist assumes that the answer to your question lies in your unconscious and your forgotten early childhood experiences and that your presented problem is only the tip of the iceberg of the "real problem." They believe that uncovering the answer is a lengthy process filled with resistance.

"I want to change who I am." or: *"I want to change my personality."*
Changing your personality, in the opinion of most therapists, is like altering the foundation and walls of your house. It requires

more work, time, and money. It is one thing to help you appreciate who you are or use your potential better. It is another matter to restructure who you are. The same applies if you wish to restructure your family in major, basic ways (like changing a totally enmeshed family into one with clear boundaries) or change somebody else's personality. Any attempt to change somebody else can be both lengthy and frustrating.

"I want to be more creative." or: *"I want to self-actualize myself, to become the best I can be."*

Self-actualization is another way to invite long-term therapy. Most therapists, including myself, will gladly accept you for open-ended, in-depth, "growth" therapy because you are a desirable client. You are a motivated, intelligent, and resourceful person who wants to use therapy beyond problem solving. Don't expect the therapist to end such therapy soon.

"I wish to heal a trauma of my past."

This is a very common request of the psychologically-minded person, as well as of those who were severely abused by toxic parents. This is an up-front request for long-term therapy and indeed an appropriate one, since parents have great influence on everyone and there is very little anyone can do to reverse the history of their upbringing or change their parents. Parental influence is a very heavy and complex load to carry alone.

"I need somebody to understand me better than (for example) my spouse or my parents do."

You are looking for a therapist to replace an inadequate or missing figure in your life or at least provide you with a corrective experience. Let's say you had an aloof and unavailable father and you are looking for a warm and available therapist to pay close attention to you. Or your spouse never seems to listen to you and you come to therapy to get an attentive and patient listener. If the therapist enters symbolically into this role, you can expect a lengthy therapy. It is a very complex venture. The core of long-term therapy is handling the transference of feelings and major disappointments onto the figure of the therapist.

The more generic and vague the goal in therapy is, the harder it will be to know when it's over. Often, therapy lingers on simply because it has become a habit or a weekly ritual without any definite goal. You can always find something to talk about with a therapist, especially if she or he is a good, empathetic listener who is supportive of you. Making something bad okay is easier than making something that is 75 percent okay into something that is 100 percent okay. It is harder because life always produces ups and downs that keep people from reaching the 100-percent spot permanently.

In dealing with past traumas, therapy will be shorter only when you fully realize that there is little or nothing that can be done to change the reality of your past or your parents. It is important to recognize that, to acknowledge your feelings about it, and reconstruct some of your memories. Whatever you do, eventually you need to forgive your parents and yourself (again and again) so you can go on with your life. By the way, such a process can be done in a self-help group with people who have gone through similar experiences, but it may not be effective to do group therapy within a time limit.

If you are paying for therapy, you certainly want to get your money's worth. Each therapeutic goal requires a different amount of time, money, and effort. Each solution carries its own promises as well as risks. You need to address those risks by first asking yourself how and how soon you expect to be helped. Let the therapist know in the first phone call and make sure to ask about how and how soon she or he may be able to help you. If the answer is something along the lines of: "There is no way for me to know until I see you," or "Let's cross that bridge when we get to it," you can still find out what experience she or he has had with other clients like you, including length of treatment. If at the end of this brief conversation, you are unclear and vague about your future therapy, my advice is to do some more homework before you start therapy. Take a little more time to clarify your goals for yourself. Your alternatives will be to call another therapist, or to talk it over with a friend who has been in therapy, or talk with the person who referred you to the therapist you just called (just remember he or she is a biased observer who may want you to go to this particular therapist).

C'est la vie

From reading this book you may think I personally object to long-term therapy. I do not. I do think it should be the exception, not the rule. It should be provided in a minority of cases, and only when it is appropriate: when the client wants and needs it. I am a veteran of good long-term therapy (as a client). I did not have any bad experiences in long-term therapy because my therapists were excellent and I was using it as part of my training and development as a therapist. Moreover, to this day I tend to keep a few clients for long-term therapy. I need it. I am currently a private, fee-for-service therapist. My long-term clients help to pay my mortgage and give me the pleasure of developing an intimate affinity with people I care for and love. I'm not eager to give it all up, especially when I'm paid for doing what I love most (meeting with and listening to people). If I limit my practice to single-session clients my neighbors will suspect I have opened a train station and I'll hardly remember the dozens of people I see every week. Besides, with such a glut of therapists around me, it is hard to generate so many new clients every week. The dilemma of the therapist is that on the one hand his or her job is to help the clients solve their problems. On the other hand, if the clients get "cured" too quickly, the therapist will not have enough business. (Don't get me wrong. The therapist's problem in making a living is not the client's problem.)

Therapy is a professional service and not a substitute for real life. Indeed, you may elect to continue therapy in order to further improve or take better care of other problems. You certainly may continue therapy as long as you have the necessary resources for it. My experience is that the law of diminishing returns begins to take hold in most therapies somewhere between the first and the tenth session. As in many other aspects of life, we seem to know better how to start than when to quit. (This decision may be forced on you by third-party payers such as insurance companies, the government, employers, and health care carriers, who are limiting the coverage of outpatient therapy to fewer and fewer sessions.)

The ultimate test of therapy is not how long it takes, but whether the therapeutic experience (like feeling hopeful) can be transferred to your everyday life and your relationships with the people with whom you share your life. Therapists are trained and paid for their ability to express warmth, support, and human understanding. Yet, your therapist can't and shouldn't replace your lover, sibling, or parent.

The wise therapist will never require you to have only one session, but will convey the possibility that together you may be able to find a good solution quickly, and in any case the door will stay open for more sessions on an as-needed basis. In this regard I like the words of my fellow therapist Dr. Michael Hoyt in his book with Simon Budman, *The First Session in Brief Therapy:* "SST is actually an open-ended form of therapy; we suggest one session may be enough to provide structure and promote change, but it is the patient who decides if one visit is sufficient."

With all I know now about the practice of psychotherapy I can't feel comfortable any more with the idea that anybody would have to pay a large portion of their income one to five times a week (for many years) in order to get sufficient attention or have a trustworthy friend or reliable parental figure. It seems to me a sad statement about Western culture, where intimate relationships, interpersonal warmth and understanding, and emotional support systems need to be formally hired.

The expense is not only the high fee for the "talking cure." It is the mental energy that is directed toward the therapist and therapy instead of being directed where it could be— toward friends, family, the communities we are a part of, ideas, projects . . . . I somehow feel that it is pretentious for therapists to think they can replace "real" people and "real" love, to believe they can offer corrective experiences that truly compensate for the absence of other people or feelings. After all, this is specifically a professional service, with clear limits of time, money, and skills.

There is also a "catch" in needing therapy in order to be independent or in needing a therapist in order to gain self-mastery. I believe you won't know how independent and autonomous you have become until you quit therapy and find out that you can do just fine without your therapist.

In short, let go of your therapist as soon as possible. Keep going on with your life by utilizing your hidden therapist, by locating and emphasizing your strengths. Don't worry. There are plenty of problems coming your way. Life is immensely complex and filled with difficult challenges. That doesn't change after SST, nor after ten years of therapy. Just take it one session, one day at a time. You will get stuck again one day. And you can always call a therapist again, especially if you trust him or her to be helpful to you, as soon as possible, in the most cost-effective way available.

Appendix

A Therapist's Introductory Letter
to a Potential Client

To My Clients:

It may be helpful to tell you how I see the job of a therapist. My job is to facilitate your psychological well-being, by helping you to solve the problem or dilemma that may have made you feel stuck and demoralized.

The first thing you need to know is that the goal of the therapist is to help you help yourself. The therapist's greatest pleasure and reward should be to see you go back to the business of life more confident of your ability to take care of your problems, trusting your judgment and intuition. Therapy should be helpful and efficient, and thus, as brief and as unintrusive as possible to your normal life. Our main allies in achieving this goal are not the latest technologies or scientific findings. They are your mental and physical abilities. The therapist is not the healer. You are! The therapist's job is to help activate and facilitate your own healing mechanism and your inner wisdom.

The therapist should never doubt that your pains and problems are real. The act of seeking the help of a psychotherapist may make you feel as if you are crazy or a hypochondriac. You are not! The therapist will learn about you by listening very carefully to everything you say and asking questions to find out what got you stuck. Why are your warning signals flashing? Most important, the therapist will search with you for ways to get you unstuck and to facilitate the necessary shift or change.

The combination of your available psychological knowledge and the wisdom of your body-mind is a powerful team and knows what to do. Muster your resources—spiritual, emotional, intellectual, physical, and social. You are not alone. Many sources of help are available to you. Do not panic or give up. Your most powerful tool is your will to live. Your coming to see a therapist is an expression of your will to live and your willingness to do whatever you need to do to recover and regain your self-mastery. Don't ask yourself to do anything unless you know that you are capable of it and that it will facilitate the necessary changes. At all times you will be in charge of the change and of the healing process. The therapist should not trick you or make you do things that may humiliate or harm you or allow you to lose control.

Although the therapist will be available and by your side whenever and as long as necessary, your job is to make the therapist obsolete as soon as possible. End therapy as soon as you feel that the problem is solved or—more likely and more precisely— that you can manage it on your own.

You are here because you want to stop the pain and regain hope. This will be the time to put into fullest use whatever capacity is left in you to enjoy and laugh. Talk with your therapist about joys as much as sorrows, about solutions as much as problems. Therapy is not a place only to complain and blame. You may have come to therapy because you feel helpless and like a victim; do not make therapy a place to do more of the same things that made you feel badly. Therapy is a place to change, take charge, regain hope, and solve problems.

No doubt you have some negative feelings right now and you should express them openly. But watch out! Negative feelings can ignite your entire mind like fire in a windy, dry summer. When negative thoughts occupy the mind, they can block out other perceptions, prospects, and pleasures.

Forgiveness is a gift you need to give not only to others but to yourself. Everyone makes plenty of mistakes and everyone needs to be forgiven in order to move on. Nothing clutters the soul more than remorse, resentment, recrimination. Guilt and blame are the best bet for not changing. The easiest way to deepen a grievance is to cling to it. The surest way to intensify a problem is to blame yourself. Change and action come more easily out of non-judgmental understanding and self-love than out of criticizing and undermining yourself.

Therapy should generate and encourage your confidence in yourself and in your capacity to solve the problem. Form a partnership of hope. Your hope, which you've displayed by coming to therapy, is the therapist's secret weapon. It is the most potent ingredient in any prescription, in any task you decide to take upon yourself.

Bibliography and Selected Sources

Andreas, Connirae, and Steve Andreas. *Heart of the Mind: Engaging Your Inner Power to Change with Neuro-Linguistic Programming.* Moab, UT: Real People Press, 1989.

Bandler, Richard, and John Grinder. *Frogs into Princes: Neuro-Linguistic Programming.* Moab, UT: Real People Press, 1979.

Bandler, Richard. *Using Your Brain—for a Change.* Moab, UT: Real People Press, 1985.

Beck, Aaron T. *Cognitive Therapy & Emotional Disorders.* New York: International Universities Press, 1976.

—.*Depression: Clinical, Experimental and Theoretical Aspects.* New York: Hoeber Medical Division, Harper & Row, 1967.

—.*Love Is Never Enough: How Couples Can Overcome Misunderstandings, Resolve Conflicts and Solve Relationship Problems through Cognitive Therapy.* New York: Harper & Row, 1988.

Beck, Aaron T., A. J. Rush, B.F. Shaw, and G. Emery. *Cognitive Therapy of Depression.* New York: Guilford Press, 1979.

Benson, Herbert, and Miriam Z. Klipper. *The Relaxation Response.* New York: William Morrow & Co., 1975.

Benson, Herbert, and William Proctor. *Beyond the Relaxation Response.* New York: New York Times Books, 1984.

Berg, Insoo, and Scott D. Miller. *Working with the Problem Drinker: A Solution-Focused Approach.* New York: W.W. Norton, 1993.

Berman, Jeffrey S., and N.C. Norton. "Does Professional Training Make a Therapist More Effective?" *Psychological Bulletin* 98, no 2 (Sept. 1985): 401–407.

Berne, E. *Principles of Group Treatment.* New York: Oxford University Press, 1966.

Bloom, Bernard L. *Community Mental Health: A General Introduction.* Monterey, CA: Brooks/Cole, 1984.

—. *Planned Short-Term Psychotherapy: A Clinical Handbook.* Needham Heights, MA: Allyn and Bacon, 1992.

Bowers, T.G., and G.A. Clum. "Relative Contribution of Specific and Nonspecific Research." *Psychological Bulletin* 103, no 3 (May 1988): 315–323.

Budman, Simon H., Michael F. Hoyt, and Steven Friedman. *The First Session in Brief Therapy.* New York: Guilford, 1992.

Burns, David D. *Feeling Good: The New Mood Therapy.* New York: Signet, 1980.

Calabrese, Joseph R., Mitchel A. Kling, and Philip W. Gold. "Alterations in Immunocompetence during Stress, Bereavement, and Depression: Focus on Neuroendocrine Regulation." *American Journal of Psychiatry* 144, no 9 (Sept. 1987): 1123–1134.

Cousins, Norman. *Head First: The Biology of Hope.* New York: E.P. Dutton, 1989.

Day, G. "Spellbinding and Spellbreaking in Convalescence." *Lancet* (January 27, 1962): 211–213.

de Shazer, Steve, Insoo Berg, Eve Lipchik, Elam Nunnally, A. Molnar, W. Gingerich, and M. Weiner-Davis. "Brief Therapy: Focused Solution Development." *Family Process* 25, no 2 (June 1986): 207–222.

de Shazer, Steve. *Keys to Solutions in Brief Therapy.* New York: W.W. Norton, 1985.

Endicott, Jean, Marvin Herz, and Miriam Gibbon. "Brief Versus Standard Hospitalization: The Differential Costs." *American Journal of Psychiatry* 135, no 6 (June 1978): 707–712.

Erickson, Milton H. *Conversations with Milton H. Erickson, M.D.* Edited by Jay Haley. Volume 1: *Changing Individuals.* New York: Triangle Press, Distributed by W.W. Norton, 1985.

—. *An Uncommon Case Book: The Complete Clinical Work of Milton H. Erickson, M.D.* Summarized and compiled by William H. O'Hanlon and Angela L. Hexum. New York: W.W. Norton, 1973.

Ferguson, Marilyn. *The Aquarian Conspiracy: Personal & Social Transformation in Our Time.* L.A.: J. P. Tarcher, 1980.

Fisch, Richard, J. H. Weakland, and L. Segal. *The Tactics of Change: Doing Therapy Briefly.* San Francisco: Jossey-Bass, 1983.

Frances, A., and J.F. Clarkin. "No Treatment as the Prescription of Choice." *Archives of General Psychiatry* 38, no 5 (May 1981): 542–545.

Frank, Jerome D., R. Hoehn-Saric, S. Imber, B.L. Liberman, and A.R. Stone. *Effective Ingredients of Successful Psychotherapy.* New York: Burnner/Mazel, 1978.

Frank, Jerome D., and Julia B. Frank. *Persuasion & Healing: A Comparative Study of Psychotherapy.* Baltimore, MD: Johns Hopkins University Press, 1991.

Frankl, Viktor. *Man's Search for Meaning.* New York: Touchstone, 1984.

Garfield, Sol L. *The Practice of Brief Psychotherapy.* New York: Pergamon Press, 1989.

Gergen, Kenneth J. *The Saturated Self: Dilemmas of Identity in Contemporary Life.* New York: Basic Books, 1991.

Goleman, Daniel. "When a Long Therapy Goes a Little Way." *New York Times,* April 18, 1993.

Haley, Jay. *Uncommon Therapy: The Psychiatric Techniques of Milton H. Erickson, M.D.* New York: W.W. Norton, 1973.

—. *Strategies of Psychotherapy.* New York: Grune & Stratton, 1963.

—. *Problem-Solving Therapy.* 2d ed. San Francisco: Jossey-Bass, 1987.

Hoyt, M., R. Rosenbaum, and M. Talmon. "Planned Single Session Therapy." In Budman, Simon H., Michael F. Hoyt, and Steven Friedman. *The First Session in Brief Therapy.* New York: Guilford Press, 1992.

Ingelfinger, F. "Arrogance." *New England Journal of Medicine* 303 (1980): 1506–1511.

Jung, C. G. *Memories, Dreams, Reflections.* New York: Vintage Books, Division of Random House, 1961.

Keeney, Bradford P. *Improvisational Therapy: A Practical Guide for Creative Clinical Strategies.* New York: Guilford Press, 1991.

Kojo, I. "The Mechanism of the Psychophysiological Effects of Placebo." *Medical Hypotheses* 27 (1989): 261–264.

Kooss, M.P., and J.N. Butcher. "Research on Brief Psychotherapy." In A.E. Bergin and S.L. Garfield. *Handbook of Psychotherapy and Behavior Change: An Empirical Analysis.* New York: Wiley, 1986.

Luborsky, L., B. Singer, and L. Luborsky. "Comparative Studies of Psychotherapies." *Archives of General Psychiatry* 32 (1975): 995–1008.

Luborsky, L., P. Crits-Christoph, J. Minz, and A. Auerbach. *Who Will Benefit from Psychotherapy? Predicting Therapeutic Outcomes.* New York: Basic Books, 1988.

Madanes, Cloe. *Strategic Family Therapy.* San Francisco: Jossey-Bass, 1981.

Mahoney, Michael J. *Human Change Processes: The Scientific Foundation of Psychotherapy.* New York: Basic Books, 1991.

Mann, James, and Robert Goldman. *A Casebook in Time-Limited Psychotherapy.* New York: McGraw Hill, 1982.

Mann, James. *The Time-Limited Psychotherapy.* Cambridge, MA: Harvard University Press, 1973.

Mattes, J.A., B. Rosen, and D.F. Klein. "Comparison of the Clinical Effectiveness Short Versus Long Stay Psychiatric Hospitalization. Results of Three-Year Post-Hospital Follow-up." *Journal of Nervous and Mental Disease* 165 (1977): 387–394.

McKenzie, K.R. "Recent Developments in Brief Psychotherapy." *Hospital and Community Psychiatry* 39 (1988): 742–752.

Melnechuk, T. "Emotions, Brain, Immunity, and Health: A Review." In M. Clynes and J. Panksepp, eds., *Emotions and Psychopathology.* New York: Plenum Press, 1988.

Meredith, N. "Testing the Talking Cure." *Science* 86 (June 1986): 29–37.

Nossal, G.J.V. "Current Concepts: Immunology." *The New England Journal of Medicine* 316 (1987): 1320–1325.

O'Hanlon, William H., and Michele Weiner-Davis. *In Search of Solutions: A New Directions in Psychotherapy.* New York: W.W. Norton, 1989.

Piper, William E., Elie G. Debbane, J.P. Bienvenu, and Jacques Garant. "A Comparative Study of Four Forms of Psychotherapy." *Journal of Consulting and Clinical Psychology* 52, no 2 (April 1984): 268–279.

Rabkin, R. *Strategic Psychotherapy: Brief and Symptomatic Treatment.* New York: Basic Books, 1977.

Rosen, Sidney, ed. *My Voice Will Go with You: The Teaching Tales of Milton H. Erickson, M.D.* New York: W.W. Norton, 1985.

Russell, Roberta, and R.D. Laing. *R.D. Laing & Me: Lessons in Love.* Lake Placid, New York: Hillgarth Press, 1992.

Sacks, Oliver. *The Man Who Mistook His Wife for a Hat: and Other Clinical Tales.* New York: Summit Books, 1985.

Seligman, Martin E. *Learned Optimism: How to Change Your Mind and Your Life.* New York: Alfred A. Knopf, 1990.

Shapiro, A.K. "A Contribution to the History of the Placebo Effect." *Behavioral Science* 5 (1960): 117.

Shapiro, F. "Eye Movement Desensitization & Reprocessing Procedure: From EMD to EMD/R—A New Treatment Model for Anxiety and Related Trauma." *The Behavior Therapist* (May 1991): 133–135.

Siegel, Bernard S. *Love, Medicine & Miracles.* New York: Harper & Row, 1986.

Smith, Mary L., G.V. Glass, and T.I. Miller. *The Benefits of Psychotherapy.* Baltimore, MD: Johns Hopkins University Press, 1980.

Solomon, G.F., et al. "An Intensive Psychoimmunologic Study of Long-Surviving with AIDS," *Annals of the New York Academy of Sciences* 496 (1987): 647–655.

Swartzburg, M., and A. Schwartz. "A Five Year Study of Brief Hospitalization." *American Journal of Psychiatry* 133 (1976): 922–924.

Talmon, Moshe. *Single-Session Therapy: Maximizing the Effect of the First (& Often Only) Therapeutic Encounter.* San Francisco: Jossey-Bass, 1990.

Watzlawick, Paul, J.H. Weakland, and R. Fisch. *Change: Principles of Problem Formation & Problem Resolution.* New York: W.W. Norton, 1974.

White, Michael, and David Epston. *Narrative Means to Therapeutic Ends.* New York: W.W. Norton, 1990.

Index

Index

Index

Index

Index

Index